MORE TAKEAWAY SECRETS

How to Cook More of Your Favourite Fast Food at Home

ONLINE GALLERY

To view photos of takeaway dishes made by readers of *The Takeaway Secret* and photos of recipes in this book, scan the QR code shown above with your mobile or tablet or simply enter **fug.io/ryx** into your web browser.

Also in Right Way

The Takeaway Secret★
The Curry Secret
The New Curry Secret
An Indian Housewife's Recipe Book
Chinese Cookery Secrets
Thai Cookery Secrets
Curries and Spicy Dishes for Your Slow Cooker

★Also by Kenny McGovern

www.constablerobinson.com/rightway

MORE TAKEAWAY SECRETS

HOW TO COOK MORE OF YOUR FAVOURITE FAST FOOD AT HOME

Kenny McGovern

RIGHT WAY

Constable & Robinson Ltd
55–56 Russell Square
London WC1B 4HP
www.constablerobinson.com

First published by Right Way, an imprint of Constable & Robinson, 2012

A copy of the British Library Cataloguing in Publication Data
is available from the British Library

ISBN: 978-0-7160-2300-5

Printed and bound in the EU
1 3 5 7 9 10 8 6 4 2

CONTENTS

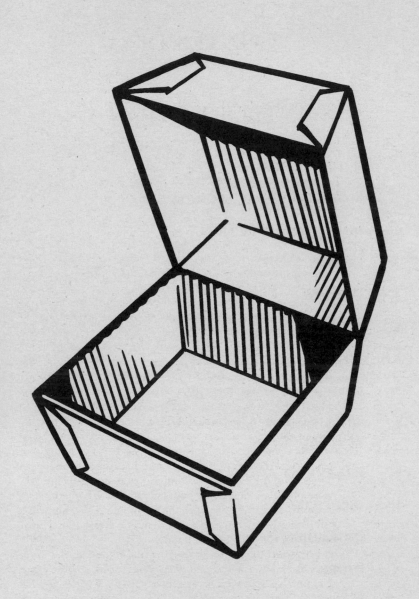

INTRODUCTION

My interest in recreating takeaway and fast-food dishes at home was one I never imagined would be shared by others. For many months and even years, I quietly worked away in my kitchen, hoping to please only myself with the dishes I cooked. What began as a fun hobby quickly progressed into something of an obsession and before long I was attempting to recreate several things every day of the week. With every success came a renewed interest in finding other dishes to recreate, to the extent that I looked forward to the newest takeaway menu coming through the letterbox in order that I could decide which new menu items I might try to cook.

As time passed I began to share my recipes with family and friends. I soon found that my interest was shared by more than a few people, particularly among those on various internet football forums who had tried and tested the recipes I passed on to them. Soon I was being sent photographs of various takeaway dishes people had made, along with requests and suggestions for other dishes I might try to create recipes for. The recipes were proving increasingly popular and so I was encouraged to put them together in a book. Initially, the book was seen simply as a further extension of my hobby, something I might create myself that could be enjoyed by a few friends and family.

Over time I was encouraged to aim higher and hope that the book may be made available to a wider audience. With thanks to the great support from Constable and Robinson, this is exactly what happened and *The Takeaway Secret* was published. I could hardly contain my excitement on its release and, with every day that has passed since its publication, I have been both humbled and amazed by how well it has been received among those people who have purchased a copy. Their support and enthusiasm for the recipes have been beyond my wildest dreams and I can't thank everyone involved enough for joining in my obsession.

In the introduction to *The Takeaway Secret* I also decided to include the real story of where my interest in cooking these widely available dishes at home had come from. I spoke about my struggle with Social Anxiety Disorder and the effect it had on my everyday life, leaving me almost housebound at times through panic attacks and severe anxiety. While the response to the recipes pleased me very much, I was also hugely delighted by the number of people who got in contact to offer words of encouragement and support in relation to my illness. Even more touching was the fact that I also received emails from people who suffer from the same illness, many of whom had purchased the book purely to enjoy cooking takeaway food and had been surprised when they recognised themselves in my description of Social Anxiety. It's been hugely helpful to me to be able to discuss the illness with so many people and I am delighted that making reference to it in the book has had such a positive effect. I still struggle with the effects of the illness to this day but am hopeful that I can continue to make progress in dealing with the difficulties it brings.

Of course, in relation to Social Anxiety Disorder, my huge thanks go to my fiancée Rebecca and my family and friends who have been constantly supportive and understanding. Their help and encouragement have been ever present both in everyday life and in the writing of these books and their influence cannot be underestimated.

Special mention should also go to Roisin and Christy, my young niece and nephew, who have been extremely helpful in taste-testing every dessert included in the book. Even when the results met with instant approval, their perfectionism demanded that the various cakes and biscuits be baked again and again, determined as they were to double and triple check every dessert dish for completely selfless reasons. Even now, with the book completed, they remain eager to carry on testing just one more time…

After the release of *The Takeaway Secret*, it could have been assumed that my interest had reached its peak. In fact, the response the book had and the many requests made for future recipes led to my obsession growing stronger than ever. Within only a few weeks I found myself back in the kitchen with a long list of dishes I had yet to fully master.

The beauty of the fast-food industry and the modern world we live in is that the range of foods increases from day to day and week to week. It's just one of many positives in a multicultural society that we learn more about the foods enjoyed around the world and as we share our lives with people of varying ethnicities and nationalities, the fast-food menu becomes ever more diverse. There is always another dish to create or another flavour to find and, on that note, I hope that you are ready to enjoy *More Takeaway Secrets*...

1

MORE TAKEAWAY SECRETS

As my interest in recreating fast food at home has grown, the number of dishes I've attempted to recreate has grown with it. My interest in takeaway dishes initially involved nothing more than frequently purchasing fast food and the number of orders I made to my local delivery restaurants very much reflected my lack of cooking ability!

I've become much more confident in the kitchen and discovered that, even when things don't go quite to plan, cooking is still a fun and enjoyable process. Many people are intimidated by the idea of cooking and this apprehension isn't helped by various TV chefs whose programmes often involve aggressive tirades and military style instructions, shouted in anger and directed at nervous and timid amateur cooks. The impression is given that cooking is extremely serious business and the slightest mistake constitutes a complete disaster.

Of course, cooking doesn't have to be this way, particularly in the home. Cooking should be a method of de-stressing, and can be very therapeutic, provided that you don't have to endure the rants of the aforementioned angry chefs! Anyone can learn to cook and create dishes that are as delicious and enjoyable as anything you could order from your local restaurants. The best way to guarantee an easy cooking experience is to ensure that all of your required ingredients are prepared and arranged before cooking begins. With vegetables chopped and sauces prepared, your attention can remain focused on the frying pan, and the process of creating your meal becomes a simple one.

Delving deeper into takeaway and fast-food menus, the number of dishes that can now be faithfully recreated at home is increased. The range includes burgers, kebabs, Indian curries, Chinese stir-fry dishes, pizzas, chip shop foods, Thai curry, Mexican chilli dishes, Japanese chicken and much more, as well as a selection of recipes which I hope will prove useful for breakfast and lunchtime meals. Under strict instruction from my fiancée, I've also made sure to include an increased number of dessert dishes!

I hope you'll enjoy cooking these meals yourself and that the results will prove successful.

Happy cooking!

2

BURGERS AND WRAPS

There are many varying opinions on the true origin of the hamburger. Many believe it to date back to the fifteenth century when minced beef was considered a delicacy throughout Europe. Others consider it to be a development of steak tartare, introduced to Germany from Russia. The vast number of German ports in the eighteenth and nineteenth centuries led to the widespread consumption of 'Hamburg steak'. Its popularity was such that many New Yorkers set up food stands along the port offering 'steak cooked in the Hamburg style' in the hope that German sailors might be attracted.

In modern terms, it is undoubtedly America's influence on the hamburger that has seen it grow to become one of the world's most widely consumed fast foods. The introduction of a consistent product, coupled with a speedy service method led to the creation of a fast-food model now mimicked across the entire industry. The simplicity of a good hamburger makes it a perfect choice for fast-food restaurants. The meat product can be (and often is) delivered frozen to restaurants, allowing for long-term storage. As fast-food hamburgers are traditionally so thin, they can be cooked from frozen in a very short time, allowing restaurants to ensure a fast turnover of customers.

The burger is equally convenient for its customer: a meal which can be quickly delivered, eaten by hand and topped with any variety of cheeses, salads and sauces. The traditional beef patty hamburger has now also been joined with a much wider variety of items so that today it's possible to order lamb, chicken or vegetable burgers served in the same way.

The hamburger is of course the primary menu item in many American fast-food restaurants but has grown in popularity to the extent where it is now a regular feature on kebab shop and chip shop menus around the country. Many kebab shops combine elements of their burger and kebabs to offer a mixed product. For example, topping your burger with sliced lamb doner meat will create what's often called a 'kismet burger', perfect if the decision between a hamburger and a kebab is proving too difficult a choice to make!

BACON DOUBLE CHEESEBURGER

(AMERICAN FAST-FOOD STYLE)

Serves 1

Roughly 113 g/4 oz beef mince (minimum 20% fat)
2 slices smoked bacon
1 burger bun
Pinch of salt and pinch of black pepper
2 processed cheese slices
½ tablespoon tomato ketchup (recommended brand: Heinz)

Divide the beef mince and roll into two equal sized balls. Using a sheet of greaseproof paper, flatten the mince into two thin, circular patties, slightly bigger than the size of your burger bun. Cover and freeze for at least 1 hour. The burger patties can be cooked from frozen.

Cook the bacon in a frying pan over a low-medium heat for 3–4 minutes or until just cooked through, turning once halfway through cooking. Remove the bacon from the pan and set aside. Or grill the bacon if desired.

Heat a dry, flat frying pan to a medium-high heat. Toast the burger buns face down in the pan for around 30 seconds or until golden. Set aside. Reduce the heat to medium. Place the burger patties onto the hot, dry pan and cook for 2 minutes. Apply very gentle pressure with a spatula to ensure even browning. Flip the burgers. Add a pinch of salt and black pepper and cook for a further 2 minutes or until cooked through and the juices run clear.

Place a cheese slice on top of each burger patty and leave the burgers in the pan for a further 30 seconds until the cheese melts slightly. Use a spatula to lift one burger patty on top of the other. Remove the burgers from the pan and set aside on a plate covered with foil to keep warm. If necessary, cook the burgers one at a time and keep warm in the oven at the lowest available setting until required.

Dress the top burger bun with ketchup. Place the cooked burgers on the bottom bun and top with the bacon. Add the dressed top bun and wrap the burger loosely in foil or baking paper. Heat through in the oven at the lowest setting for 3–4 minutes to combine flavours. Serve with French fries.

TASTY BIG BURGER

(AMERICAN FAST-FOOD STYLE)

Serves 1

Processed cheese and melted Emmental combine perfectly with the creamy sauce used to top this burger.

Roughly 113 g/4 oz beef mince (minimum 20% fat)
1 large sesame burger bun
Pinch of salt and pinch of black pepper
1 processed cheese slice
1 slice Emmental cheese (recommended brand: President)
2 raw onion ring slices
2 tomato slices
1 small handful of shredded iceberg lettuce
1 tablespoon tasty burger sauce (page 19)

Roll the beef mince into a ball. Using a sheet of greaseproof paper, flatten the mince into a thin, circular patty, slightly bigger than the size of your burger bun. Cover and freeze for at least 2 hours. The burger patties can be cooked from frozen.

Heat a flat, dry frying pan to a medium-high heat. Toast the burger buns face down in the pan for around 30 seconds or until golden. Set aside.

Place the burger patty onto the hot, dry frying pan and cook for 2–3 minutes. Apply very gentle pressure with a spatula to ensure even browning. Flip the burger. Add a pinch of salt and pepper and cook for a further 2 minutes or until cooked through and the juices run clear.

Place the processed cheese slice on the bottom bun. Place the cooked burger patty on top. Dress the burger patty with the Emmental cheese slice, raw onion slices, tomato slices and shredded iceberg lettuce.

Dress the top burger bun with the tablespoon of tasty burger sauce and place on top. Wrap the burger loosely in foil or baking paper and place in the oven at the lowest available setting for 2–3 minutes to combine flavours and heat through. Serve with French fries.

WHOPPING BIG BURGER

(AMERICAN FAST-FOOD STYLE)

Serves 1

It's all in the assembly when it comes to this classic burger, fit for a king!

Roughly 113 g/4 oz beef mince (minimum 20% fat)
1 large sesame seed burger bun
Pinch of salt and pinch of black pepper
1 tablespoon mayonnaise (recommended brand: Hellman's)
1 small handful of shredded iceberg lettuce
1 tablespoon tomato ketchup (recommended brand: Heinz)
4 thin slices of gherkin
2 raw onion ring slices
2 tomato slices

Roll the beef mince into a ball. Using a sheet of greaseproof paper, flatten the mince into a thin, circular patty, slightly bigger than the size of your burger bun. Cover and place in the coldest part of the fridge for 1–2 hours. The burger patty may also be frozen if desired.

Heat a griddle pan to a medium-high heat. Toast the burger buns face down in the pan for around 30 seconds or until golden. Set aside.

Place the burger patty onto the hot, dry griddle pan and cook for 2–3 minutes. Apply very gentle pressure with a spatula to ensure even browning. Flip the burger. Add a pinch of salt and pepper and cook for a further 2 minutes or until cooked through and juices run clear.

Spread the mayonnaise on the top burger bun and add the shredded lettuce. Place the burger patty onto the bottom bun and dress with the tomato ketchup, gherkin slices, raw onion ring slices and tomato slices.

Place the top bun on top of the dressed bottom bun. Wrap the burger loosely in foil or baking paper and place in the oven at the lowest available setting for 3–4 minutes to combine flavours and heat through. Serve with French fries.

TEX-MEX BURGER

(KEBAB SHOP STYLE)

Serves 1

Roughly 113 g/4 oz beef mince (minimum 20% fat)
¼ teaspoon Cajun spice mix (page 186)
½ teaspoon Worcester sauce
2 tablespoons finely chopped onion
1 small garlic clove, crushed
Pinch of salt and pinch of black pepper
1 large sesame seed burger bun
1 tablespoon mayonnaise, mixed with a small pinch of Cajun
  spice mix
1 small handful shredded iceberg lettuce
1 processed cheese slice
1 tablespoon jarred jalapeno peppers, patted dry with kitchen
  paper and chopped

In a small bowl, combine the mince, Cajun spice mix, Worcester sauce, onion, garlic, salt and pepper. Mix well until thoroughly combined.

Roll the mince into a ball. Using a sheet of greaseproof paper, flatten the mince into a thin, circular patty, slightly bigger than the size of your burger bun. Cover and place in the coldest part of the fridge for 1–2 hours. The burger patty may also be frozen if desired.

Heat a griddle pan to a medium-high heat. Toast the burger buns face down in the pan for around 30 seconds or until golden. Set aside. Place the burger patty onto the hot, dry griddle pan and cook for 2–3 minutes. Apply very gentle pressure with a spatula to ensure even browning. Flip the burger. Add a little extra salt and pepper and cook for a further 2 minutes or until cooked through and juices run clear.

Spread the mayonnaise on the top burger bun and add the shredded lettuce. Place the processed cheese slice on the bottom bun. Place the burger patty on top of the cheese-topped bun and add the chopped jalapeno peppers.

Place the top bun on top of the dressed bottom bun. Wrap the burger loosely in foil or baking paper and heat through in the oven at the lowest available setting for 3–4 minutes to combine flavours. Serve with French fries.

CLASSIC CHICKEN BURGER

(KEBAB SHOP STYLE)

Serves 1

This uses old school preparation techniques to create the classic chicken texture found in kebab shop chicken burgers. While the texture is the same, you have the added bonus of knowing that your burgers contain 100 per cent white breast meat. The minced chicken mixture may also be formed into small nuggets if desired.

**1 small skinless, boneless chicken breast fillet (around 85 g/
    3 oz weight)**
Pinch of salt and pinch of black pepper
1 egg
50 ml/2 fl oz semi-skimmed milk
4 tablespoons plain flour
4 tablespoons panko breadcrumbs (page 181)
½ teaspoon garlic powder
Pinch of onion powder
¼ teaspoon paprika
¼ teaspoon dried Italian herbs
Pinch of Chinese 5-spice
Pinch of cayenne pepper
½ teaspoon salt
Pinch of black pepper
1 large sesame seed burger bun
1 tablespoon mayonnaise (recommended brand: Hellman's)
1 small handful shredded iceberg lettuce

Trim any excess fat from the chicken breast and cut into 3–4 pieces. Place the chicken pieces in a blender with a little salt and pepper and blitz until minced.

In a small bowl, combine the egg and semi-skimmed milk. Whisk thoroughly and set aside.

In a large bowl, combine the plain flour, breadcrumbs, garlic powder, onion powder, paprika, dried Italian herbs, Chinese 5-spice, cayenne pepper, salt and black pepper. Mix thoroughly.

Form the minced chicken into a ball. Dip the chicken into the egg and milk mixture, and then into the seasoned coating. Set the coated chicken aside on a large plate.

Press down gently on the coated chicken to form a large patty, slightly bigger than the size of your burger bun. Set aside.

Heat a dry, flat frying pan on a medium-high heat. Toast the burger buns face down on the pan for around 30 seconds or until golden. Remove and set aside.

Shallow fry the chicken burger on a medium heat for 2–3 minutes per side, or until golden and cooked through.

Dress the top burger bun with mayonnaise and shredded lettuce.

Place the cooked chicken burger on top, add the bottom burger, flip and serve with chips.

TASTY BURGER SAUCE

(AMERICAN FAST-FOOD STYLE)

Makes enough sauce for 1 Tasty Big Burger

1 tablespoon mayonnaise (recommended brand: Hellman's)
½ teaspoon American mustard (recommended brand: French's)
½ teaspoon tomato ketchup (recommended brand: Heinz)
Dash of liquid smoke

In a small bowl, combine the mayonnaise, American mustard, tomato ketchup and liquid smoke.

Mix thoroughly and stand for 10 minutes before use.

CHICKPEA BURGER

(Kebab Shop Style)

Makes 2 Quarter-Pounder Chickpea Burgers

Crispy on the outside, moist and full of flavour on the inside, these meat-free chickpea burgers are superb served as below, or can be used as a substitute for any of the meat-based burgers in this chapter.

1 x 400 g/14 oz tin chickpeas
1 garlic clove, crushed
½ teaspoon cumin powder
¼ teaspoon coriander powder
Pinch of cayenne pepper
⅓ teaspoon salt
Pinch of black pepper
2–3 tablespoons gram flour, plus a little extra for dusting
2 large sesame seed burger buns
2 tablespoons tomato ketchup (recommended brand: Heinz)
2 tablespoons mayonnaise (recommended brand: Hellman's)
2 small handfuls shredded iceberg lettuce
Oil for deep frying

In a large pot, combine the chickpeas, garlic, cumin powder, coriander powder, cayenne pepper, salt and black pepper. Crush the mixture thoroughly with a potato masher until it becomes smooth.

Add the gram flour and mix thoroughly once again. Dust your hands with gram flour and form half of the mixture into a large ball. Compress the mixture into a large burger patty and arrange on a plate. Repeat the process with the remaining mixture so that 2 burger patties have been formed.

Arrange both the burger patties side by side on a plate and cover with cling-film. Set aside in the fridge for at least 2 hours, or overnight if possible. This will help the burgers to stay together as they cook.

Heat a dry, flat frying pan to a medium heat. Toast the burger buns face down in the pan for around 30 seconds or until golden. Set aside to cool for 30 seconds. Dress the top buns with tomato ketchup and mayonnaise and add the shredded iceberg lettuce.

Heat the oil for deep-frying over a medium heat. Keep the burger patties in the fridge until ready to be cooked.

Deep-fry the chickpea burgers for 3–4 minutes or until crisp and golden. Remove from the pan, drain off any excess oil and place on top of the dressed burger buns. Add the bottom buns. Wrap the burgers in foil or baking paper, flip and place in the oven at the lowest available setting for 3–4 minutes to combine flavours and heat through. Serve with French fries.

BARBECUE PORK BURGER

(AMERICAN FAST-FOOD STYLE)

Serves 1

This cult classic sandwich is a limited edition menu item, now available in your home all year round! Using a ridged griddle pan when forming the burger patty helps to imitate the 'rib' effect used by fast-food chains.

Roughly 56 g/2 oz pork mince
Pinch of salt and pinch of black pepper
Pinch of white sugar
1 burger bun
2 tablespoons barbecue sauce (recommended brand: Heinz)
1 teaspoon vegetable oil
½ small onion, finely sliced
4 thin slices of gherkin

Add the mince, salt, pepper and sugar to a bowl. Using slightly wet hands, mix thoroughly and roll the mixture into a ball. Lay a sheet of greaseproof paper over a ridged griddle pan. Flatten the mixture on the paper into a thin, circular patty, slightly bigger than the size of the burger bun. Carefully remove the patty and paper and freeze for at least 1 hour. The prepared pork patty can be frozen for up to 1 month and cooked from frozen.

Heat a dry, flat frying pan to a medium heat. Toast the burger buns face down in it for about 30 seconds or until golden. Allow the toasted buns to cool slightly. Spread 1 tablespoon of barbecue sauce on the bottom bun.

Add the oil to a flat frying pan and heat to a low-medium heat. Add the frozen pork patty and cook for 5–6 minutes or until just cooked through, turning occasionally and applying gentle pressure to ensure even browning. Just before the patty is cooked, brush generously with the remaining barbecue sauce on both sides and allow to cook for a further 30 seconds.

Place the cooked pork patty on top of the bottom bun. Top with the finely sliced onion and gherkin slices. Add a little more barbecue sauce if desired. Add the top bun and wrap the burger in foil or baking paper. Place in the oven at the lowest available setting for 2–3 minutes to combine flavours and heat through. Serve with French fries.

SWEET CHILLI CHICKEN WRAP

(AMERICAN FAST-FOOD STYLE)

Serves 1–2

6 tablespoons panko breadcrumbs (page 181)
¼ teaspoon salt
Pinch of black pepper
½ teaspoon garlic powder
¼ teaspoon paprika
1 teaspoon dried Italian herbs
1 large skinless, boneless chicken breast fillet (around 113 g/
    4 oz weight)
6 tablespoons plain flour
1 egg, mixed with 4 tablespoons semi-skimmed milk
Oil for deep frying
2 large flour tortillas
1 tablespoon sweet chilli sauce (page 183)
1 tablespoon mayonnaise (recommended brand: Hellman's)
6 thin slices cucumber
1 small handful shredded iceberg lettuce

In a large bowl, combine the panko breadcrumbs, salt, black pepper, garlic powder, paprika and dried Italian herbs. Mix well and set aside.

Trim any excess fat from the chicken breast and cut into 6 strips. Keeping one hand dry, dip the chicken strips first into the plain flour, then into the egg and milk mixture and finally into the prepared seasoned breadcrumbs.

Fry the chicken strips in hot oil on a medium-high heat for around 5–6 minutes or until golden brown and cooked through. Remove the chicken strips from the pan and drain off any excess oil. Set aside on a plate covered with foil to keep warm.

Heat a dry, flat frying pan over a high heat. Place the flour tortillas into the pan and cook for around 30–40 seconds, turning frequently until the tortillas are heated through.

Divide the sweet chilli sauce and mayonnaise over the middle of the tortilla wraps. Add 3 cucumber slices to each wrap. Add the shredded iceberg lettuce. Add 3 cooked chicken strips to each tortilla, wrap and serve.

BBQ STEAK WRAP

(American Fast-Food Style)

Serves 1–2

Roughly 113 g/4 oz sirloin beef steak
½ teaspoon rice wine vinegar
1 teaspoon oyster sauce
½ teaspoon soy sauce (recommended brand: Kikkoman)
Pinch of black pepper
½ teaspoon cornflour
½ green pepper, sliced
½ red pepper, sliced
1 small onion, sliced
2 large flour tortillas or tava chapatis (page 118)
1 processed cheese slice
2 tablespoons barbecue sauce (recommended brand: Heinz)

Trim any excess fat from the sirloin steak and cut into thin slices. Place in a bowl with the rice wine vinegar, oyster sauce, soy sauce and black pepper. Mix well. Add the cornflour and mix well once again. Set aside for 5 minutes.

Heat a little oil in a frying pan over a medium-high heat. Add the green pepper, red pepper and onion. Stir-fry for 3–4 minutes or until the vegetables just begin to char.

Add a touch more oil to the pan and add the marinated steak slices. Stir-fry for around 2 minutes or until the steak slices are just cooked through.

Remove the steak and vegetables from the pan and set aside on a plate covered with foil.

Heat a dry, flat frying pan over a medium-high heat. Add the flour tortillas or chapatis and cook for around 30–40 seconds, turning occasionally until the breads are heated through.

Divide the cheese slice between the breads. Add the cooked steak and vegetables. Top each tortilla with a tablespoon of barbecue sauce, wrap and serve.

3

KEBABS

In fast-food terms, the humble kebab has been given a bad press over the years. Often described in various negative terms, it is increasingly seen as the food choice of the drunk, the student or the drunk student! Labelled a high fat, high salt, poor quality meat dish, it often finds itself criticised in the pages of mainstream newspapers and magazines, many of which offer a whole host of reasons as to why it should be avoided at all costs!

Although not without an element of truth, much of the criticism is unwarranted, particularly with the recent rise of high quality independent shops, more and more of which are turning away from factory made products and instead producing their own kebabs in-house, often with an excellent list of ingredients and products. This recent trend in good quality offerings brings the fast-food kebab much closer to its origins. Freshly cooked flatbreads, topped with grilled marinated meats and finished with a selection of fresh salads and sauces create the perfect balanced meal which, prepared properly, can be enjoyed on a regular basis with only positive effects on your health.

The recipes included in this chapter include a mix of those flavours used by kebab wholesalers and a selection of recipes that reflect the new push towards more authentic dishes in takeaway and fast-food restaurants around the country. Of course, the cooking methods used by professional chefs will differ from those available in the home, so we'll use equipment more commonly available to help create the dishes as faithfully as possible.

When cooking kebabs at home, one of the best alternatives to a charcoal grill is a good quality, heavy griddle pan. When fully pre-heated, these pans will impart a smoky flavour to meats and vegetables while cooking, also adding delicious grill marks to your food. Of course, there's nothing like the real thing and, where possible, use of a charcoal grill or barbecue is preferred. However, a good quality griddle pan provides an excellent alternative for everyday cooking.

As well as a ridged griddle pan, a good quality, heavy, flat frying pan is also very useful when preparing kebabs at home. With a good heat, thinly sliced kebab meat can be treated almost like a stir-fry dish, cooked quickly to ensure the meat remains juicy and tender while the outside turns just a little charred and crispy.

Flat metal skewers are ideal for minced meat kebabs as they offer a more stable platform for the meat. Wooden skewers may also be used, provided that they have been soaked in cold water for at least 30 minutes before use in order to prevent burning.

MEDITERRANEAN
LAMB DONER KEBAB

(KEBAB SHOP STYLE)

Serves 4–6

½ teaspoon plain flour
2 teaspoons garlic powder
2 teaspoons onion powder
¼ teaspoon coriander powder
1½ teaspoons paprika
3 teaspoons cayenne pepper
1½ teaspoons dried oregano
½ teaspoon dried Italian herbs
2 teaspoons salt
¼ teaspoon black pepper
1 kg/2.2 lb lamb mince

In a large bowl, combine the plain flour, garlic powder, onion powder, coriander powder, paprika, cayenne pepper, dried oregano, dried Italian herbs, salt and black pepper. Mix well.

Add the mince and mix the ingredients thoroughly. Using slightly wet hands, knead the mixture with your fist and work it together for 2–3 minutes until the texture is completely smooth and the spices are evenly mixed.

Preheat the oven to 180°C/350°F/Gas Mark 4. Shape the doner kebab into a long loaf, the length of a baking tray. Place into the preheated oven on the middle shelf and bake for 40 minutes. Turn the doner kebab over to ensure even browning and bake for a further 40 minutes.

Remove the kebab meat from the oven and wrap tightly in foil. Set aside for 5 minutes. This will ensure the doner kebab remains soft and moist. Remove the foil and allow the kebab to cool completely. Thinly slice the kebab meat and serve with onion salad (page 125) and house special chilli sauce (page 149).

If desired, the doner kebab loaf may be cooled in the fridge overnight or frozen before slicing. The chilled meat can be sliced thinner and reheated in a dry pan until piping hot before serving.

SHAMI KEBAB

(INDIAN RESTAURANT STYLE)

Serves 3–4

1 onion, finely chopped
1 teaspoon garlic powder
½ teaspoon ginger powder
1½ teaspoons cumin powder
Pinch of coriander powder
½ teaspoon turmeric
½ teaspoon chilli powder
Pinch of paprika
1 heaped teaspoon dried fenugreek leaves
125 g/4 oz gram flour (also known as chickpea flour)
500 g/1.1 lb lamb mince

In a large bowl, combine the chopped onion, garlic powder, ginger powder, cumin powder, coriander powder, turmeric, chilli powder, paprika, dried fenugreek leaves and gram flour. Mix well.

Add the lamb mince and mix the ingredients together thoroughly. Using slightly wet hands, knead the seasoned mince mixture with your fist and work it together for 2–3 minutes until the texture is completely smooth and the spices and gram flour are evenly mixed.

Divide the mince mixture into 8 balls. Press down gently to form small burger shaped patties. Arrange the kebabs on a grill tray.

Preheat the grill to medium-high. Place the kebabs under the grill for 6–8 minutes or until cooked through, turning occasionally.

Serve the kebabs with tava chapatis (page 118) and onion salad (page 125).

BEEF SHISH KEBAB
(Kebab Shop Style)

Serves 1–2

1 tablespoon olive oil
1 tablespoon lemon juice or lemon dressing
1 teaspoon cumin powder
½ teaspoon paprika
Pinch of black pepper
½ teaspoon hot chilli flakes
1 small handful fresh coriander, finely chopped
1 small handful fresh parsley, finely chopped
1 garlic clove, crushed
½ small onion, very finely chopped
250 g/½ lb sirloin beef steak
¼ teaspoon salt
1 onion, chopped
½ red pepper, chopped
½ green pepper, chopped

In a large bowl or food-safe bag, combine the olive oil, lemon juice or lemon dressing, cumin powder, paprika, black pepper, hot chilli flakes, fresh coriander, fresh parsley, garlic and onion. Mix thoroughly and set aside.

Trim any excess fat from the beef and cut into several medium-large pieces. Add the beef pieces to the marinade, mix well by hand and marinade in the fridge for 3–4 hours, mixing the meat occasionally.

Remove the beef from the fridge 30 minutes before cooking. Add the salt and mix well. Heat a dry griddle pan to a medium-high heat. Place the chopped onion, red pepper and green pepper onto the griddle pan. Brush with a little olive oil. Wipe off any excess marinade from the beef pieces. Place the beef onto the griddle and leave for 2 minutes. Turn the beef pieces and cook along with the vegetables for a further 2–3 minutes or until just charred and cooked through.

Remove the beef from the pan and arrange on a plate. Cover with foil and allow the kebab pieces to rest for 3–4 minutes before serving with pitta or tava chapati bread (page 118), onion salad (page 125) and kebab sauces.

PORK GYROS KEBAB

(KEBAB SHOP STYLE)

Serves 1–2

1 tablespoon olive oil
75 ml/2½ fl oz red wine
1 garlic clove, crushed
1 teaspoon dried thyme
½ teaspoon dried oregano
Pinch of cinnamon
2 pork loin steaks (around 113 g/4 oz weigh per steak)
½ teaspoon of salt
Pinch of black pepper

In a large bowl or food-safe bag, combine the olive oil, red wine, garlic, dried thyme, dried oregano and cinnamon. Mix well.

Cut the pork into several medium-large pieces. Add the pork pieces to the marinade, mix well by hand and marinade for 3–4 hours, or overnight if possible, in the fridge.

Remove the pork from the fridge 30 minutes before cooking. Add the salt and pepper and mix well.

Heat a dry griddle pan to a medium-high heat. Wipe off any excess marinade from the pork pieces. Place the pork onto the griddle and leave for 2 minutes.

Turn the pork pieces and cook for a further 5–6 minutes or until charred on all sides and cooked through.

Remove the pork from the pan and serve with tortilla wraps, tava chapatis (page 118) and onion salad (page 125).

CHICKEN TIKKA DONER KEBAB

(KEBAB SHOP STYLE)

Serves 1–2

2 tablespoons natural yogurt
1 tablespoon tikka paste (recommended brand: Patak's)
¼ teaspoon garlic and ginger paste (page 182)
1 tablespoon vegetable oil
¼ teaspoon mint sauce
½ teaspoon restaurant spice mix (page 181)
Pinch of chilli powder
½ teaspoon dried fenugreek leaves
¼ teaspoon salt
4 tablespoons water
1 teaspoon natural red food colouring (optional)
4 medium skinless, boneless chicken thighs (around 226 g/
    8 oz total weight)
1 teaspoon vegetable oil

In a large bowl or food-safe bag, combine the natural yogurt, tikka paste, garlic and ginger paste, vegetable oil, mint sauce, restaurant spice mix, chilli powder, dried fenugreek leaves, salt and water. Add the natural red food colouring if desired. Mix well.

Trim any excess fat from the chicken thighs and cut each thigh into two large pieces. Add the chicken pieces to the marinade and mix well. Marinade for at least 4 hours, or overnight if possible, in the fridge.

Heat a dry, flat frying pan to a medium heat. Add the vegetable oil and carefully drop the chicken pieces into the pan. Cook for 10–12 minutes or until the chicken is golden and just cooked through. Turn the chicken pieces once halfway through the cooking time.

Remove the chicken from the pan and slice into thin strips using a knife and fork. Heat the frying pan to a high heat. Return the chicken slices to the pan and stir-fry for a further 30 seconds until just charred and piping hot.

Remove the chicken tikka doner from the pan and serve with pitta or tava chapati bread (page 118), onion salad (page 125) and kebab sauces.

MEDITERRANEAN CHICKEN DONER KEBAB

(KEBAB SHOP STYLE)

Serves 1–2

This classic chicken doner soaks up a marinade based on the one used by many kebab wholesalers and sold in thousands of kebab shops around the UK.

75 ml/2½ fl oz semi-skimmed milk
1 tablespoon olive oil
Pinch of salt
Pinch of black pepper
1 teaspoon paprika
2 garlic cloves, crushed
1 teaspoon tomato purée
2 teaspoons soy sauce
¾ teaspoon hot Madras curry powder (recommended brand: TRS)
1 teaspoon dried thyme
½ teaspoon dried oregano
1 teaspoon natural red food colouring (optional)
4 medium skinless, boneless chicken thighs (around 226 g/ 8 oz total weight)
1 teaspoon vegetable oil

In a large bowl or food-safe bag, add the semi-skimmed milk, olive oil, salt, black pepper, paprika, garlic, tomato purée, soy sauce, hot Madras curry powder, dried thyme and dried oregano. Add the natural red food colouring if desired. Mix well.

Trim any excess fat from the chicken thighs and cut each thigh into two large pieces. Add the chicken pieces to the marinade and mix well. Marinade for at least 4 hours, or overnight if possible, in the fridge.

Heat a dry, flat frying pan to a medium heat. Add the vegetable oil and carefully drop the chicken pieces into the pan. Cook for 10 –12 minutes or until the chicken is golden and just cooked through. Turn the chicken pieces once halfway through the cooking time.

Remove the chicken from the pan and slice into thin strips using a knife and fork.

Heat the frying pan to a high heat. Return the chicken slices to the pan and stir-fry for a further 30 seconds until just charred and piping hot.

Remove the chicken from the pan and serve with pitta or tava chapatis (page 118), onion salad (page 125) and kebab sauces.

SARBENI KEBAB

(KEBAB SHOP STYLE)

Serves 1

This famous dish is based on 'Lahmacun' (Turkish pizza). Many kebab shops now offer this bread as an alternative to pitta and nan bread with generous portions of kebab meat, salad and sauce.

100 g/3½ oz plain flour
50 g/2 oz wholemeal bread flour
¼ teaspoon white sugar
¼ teaspoon active dried yeast
¼ teaspoon salt
1 tablespoon olive oil
around 60 ml/2 fl oz water
roughly 56 g/2 oz beef or lamb mince
2 tablespoons red pepper, green pepper and onion, finely
    chopped
1 garlic clove, crushed
Pinch of paprika
Pinch of dried parsley
Pinch of salt and pinch of black pepper
1 small handful grated mozzarella cheese

In a large bowl, combine the plain flour, wholemeal bread flour, sugar, yeast, salt and olive oil. Mix well.

Slowly add the water until the dough comes together. Flour a work surface and pour the dough out. Knead thoroughly for 3–4 minutes or until the dough becomes smooth. Shape the dough into a ball, return to the bowl and cover with oiled cling film. Set aside for around 1 hour or until doubled in size.

In a small bowl, combine the beef or lamb mince, pepper and onion mix, garlic, paprika, dried parsley, salt and black pepper. Mix well.

Roll the dough out to around 25 cm/10 inches in size on a floured surface using a rolling pin. Lightly oil a pizza screen or tray and place the dough on top.

Carefully press the prepared mince mixture onto the top of the dough until completely covered.

Preheat the oven to 200°C/400°F/Gas Mark 6. Preheat a pizza stone in the oven if desired.

Place the pizza screen or tray into the oven and cook for 8–10 minutes or until the dough becomes crispy around the edges and the meat is cooked through. Add the mozzarella cheese to the bread and continue cooking for a further minute or until the cheese just begins to melt.

Remove the sarbeni bread from the oven and immediately top with the cooked beef or lamb kebabs. Top with chilli sauce (page 149) and onion salad (page 125). Serve the sarbeni kebab in the traditional pizza way, or roll the bread around the toppings to create an extra large kebab wrap.

CHICKEN SHAWARMA

(KEBAB SHOP STYLE)

Serves 1

2 teaspoons tomato ketchup
1 teaspoon olive oil
Dash of white vinegar
2 tablespoons lemon juice or lemon dressing
¼ teaspoon salt
½ teaspoon garlic powder
Pinch of ginger powder
¼ teaspoon paprika
Pinch of allspice
¼ teaspoon dried oregano
Pinch of dried thyme
1 large skinless, boneless chicken breast fillet (around 113 g/
    4 oz total weight)
1 large flour tortilla or tava chapati bread (page 118)
1 tablespoon garlic and herb dip (page 149)
1 small handful fresh parsley, chopped
1 small tomato, sliced
½ small onion, finely sliced

In a large bowl or food-safe bag, combine the tomato ketchup, olive oil, vinegar, lemon juice or lemon dressing, salt, garlic powder, ginger powder, paprika, allspice, oregano and thyme. Mix thoroughly.

Trim any excess fat from the chicken breast and cut into small, thin strips. Add the chicken pieces to the marinade and mix well. Marinade for 30 minutes.

Heat a dry, flat frying pan to a high heat. Add a little olive oil. Carefully drop the chicken pieces into the pan and leave untouched for 1 minute.

Stir-fry the chicken pieces for 3–4 minutes or until charred and cooked through.

Warm the flour tortilla or tava chapati bread if desired. Spread the garlic dip over the bread and top with the parsley, tomato and onion. Add the cooked shawarma chicken, wrap and serve.

4

CHINESE

In some cases, recreating takeaway or fast-food restaurant dishes at home requires us to find alternative cooking methods. It's unlikely that home cooks will be able to rely on charcoal grills, clay or pizza ovens. While we can of course produce some excellent results using these alternatives, mimicking Chinese takeaway dishes offers us the chance to cook using almost exactly the same equipment the chef would use in your local restaurant.

The equipment and utensils needed to create Chinese takeaway dishes at home are easy and inexpensive to purchase. Using just a few items, almost every dish on the menu can be recreated with ease in your own kitchen. In fact, if desired it would not be impossible to fill your kitchen with precisely the same equipment used in your local restaurant with perhaps only one minor difference. The heat level achieved in a restaurant kitchen (using gas burners, etc) is likely to be far higher than that which your home oven or hob will manage. It's often assumed that this lack of heat will lead to a lesser flavour being achieved but in Chinese dishes this is rarely the case. Your meals may take a little longer to cook at home than in a restaurant kitchen, the flavours produced however should be very similar, provided that the ingredients and cooking methods have been followed.

The most important item for use in Chinese cooking is the wok. A good quality, well seasoned wok will last a lifetime and is said to offer improved flavour as time passes and its use increases. 'The blacker the wok, the better the flavour' is a saying which is very much believed to have some basis in fact. Provided that your wok is properly seasoned and preheated, food should not stick to the base of the pan.

As well as the many traditional woks available, modern-day non-stick wok pans will also work well. In many cases, pans of this type may be preferred by those of us who are inexperienced in cooking with a wok. Electric woks are also widely available and offer surprisingly impressive results.

Another useful utensil in Chinese cooking is the 'spider', used when deep-frying foods in order to remove the ingredients from the pan while allowing excess oil to drain back into the pan. Alternatively, a large slotted spoon may be used to good effect.

My final recommendation for use in the preparation of your Chinese meals would be to purchase good quality spatulas which are safe to use when stir-frying in your wok. With these, you can scrape and stir the ingredients in the pan regularly. This is essential when cooking on a high heat to ensure the ingredients cook well without cooking unevenly or burning in the pan.

With some basic store cupboard ingredients, the decision to create a Chinese meal can be made spontaneously. The most widely used ingredients in Chinese cooking, and those worth having to hand include:

Soy sauce
Oyster sauce
Dry sherry
Rice wine vinegar
Sweet chilli sauce (page 183)
Toasted sesame oil
Vegetable oil
Garlic (or garlic powder)
Ginger (or ginger powder)
Corn flour

BEEF IN OYSTER SAUCE

(CHINESE TAKEAWAY STYLE)

Serves 1

3 tablespoons oyster sauce
2 tablespoons water
1 x 200 g/7 oz sirloin steak
1 tablespoon dry sherry
1 teaspoon soy sauce (recommended brand: Kikkoman)
½ teaspoon toasted sesame oil
Pinch of black pepper
1 teaspoon cornflour
½ small onion, chopped
½ red pepper, chopped
3–4 mushrooms, sliced
1 spring onion, finely sliced

In a small bowl, combine the oyster sauce and water. Mix well.

Trim any excess fat from the beef and slice into thin pieces. Add the dry sherry, soy sauce, toasted sesame oil and black pepper. Mix well by hand and set aside for 5 minutes.

Add the cornflour to the beef and mix well once again.

Heat a wok or frying pan to a high heat. Add a little vegetable oil. Drop the beef slices into the pan and leave for 30 seconds to seal. Stir-fry the beef for around 1–2 minutes or until just cooked through. Remove and set aside.

Add a little more oil to the pan. Add the onion, red pepper and mushrooms. Stir-fry for 2–3 minutes.

Return the beef to the pan and pour in the prepared oyster sauce and water. Mix well and cook for a further 1–2 minutes or until the sauce just begins to thicken.

Pour the beef and vegetables into a long foil tray. Garnish with sliced spring onion and serve with egg fried rice or plain chow mein.

SALT AND PEPPER CHILLI CHICKEN
(Chinese Takeaway Style)

Serves 1

½ red pepper, sliced
½ green pepper, sliced
1 finger chilli pepper, sliced (see page 62)
1 onion, sliced
2 garlic cloves, sliced
1 large skinless, boneless chicken breast fillet (around 113 g/
    4 oz weight)
Pinch of salt and pinch of black pepper
1 egg
4 tablespoons cornflour
Oil for deep frying
¾ teaspoon salt and pepper seasoning (page 183)
Dash of toasted sesame oil

In a small bowl, combine the red pepper, green pepper, chilli pepper, onion and garlic. Set aside.

Trim any excess fat from the chicken breast and cut into small pieces. Add the salt and black pepper. Mix well.

Whisk the egg in a bowl. Put the cornflour in a separate bowl.

Put the chicken pieces into the egg and mix thoroughly. Lift the chicken pieces out, allowing any excess egg to drain between your fingers. Drop the chicken pieces into the cornflour and mix thoroughly until completely dry and well coated.

Fry the chicken pieces in hot oil for 3–4 minutes or until golden brown and cooked through. Remove from the pan, drain off any excess oil and set aside. If desired, the chicken may be cooked ahead and refried briefly in hot oil a second time. Doing so will make the chicken pieces extra crispy.

When ready to finish the dish, add a little oil to a separate wok or frying pan. Add the prepared vegetables and stir-fry over a high heat for 2–3 minutes.

Add the chicken pieces to the pan with the vegetables and mix well. Add the salt and pepper seasoning and continue to stir-fry for a further minute.

Switch off the heat and add the toasted sesame oil. Mix well once more and serve as a starter or with egg fried rice/plain chow mein as a main meal.

CHICKEN WITH THIN CRISPY NOODLES

(CHINESE TAKEAWAY STYLE)

Serves 1

1 tablespoon oyster sauce
1 teaspoon soy sauce
50 ml/2 fl oz Chinese stock (page 185) or water
Pinch of black pepper
1 nest of egg noodles
½ teaspoon toasted sesame oil
1 large skinless, boneless chicken breast fillet (around 113 g/
    4 oz weight)
½ teaspoon soy sauce (recommended brand: Kikkoman)
¼ teaspoon garlic powder
Pinch of ginger powder
1 teaspoon vegetable oil plus extra for frying
1 teaspoon cornflour
½ small onion, sliced
1 small handful bean sprouts

In a small bowl, combine the oyster sauce, soy sauce, stock or water and black pepper. Mix well and set aside.

Drop the egg noodles into boiling water and simmer for 2–3 minutes, stirring well to separate the noodles. Rinse thoroughly under cold water and drain well. Toss with sesame oil and set aside.

Trim any excess fat from the chicken breast and cut into small, thin strips. Add the soy sauce, garlic powder, ginger powder and 1 teaspoon of vegetable oil. Mix well and marinade for 5 minutes. Add 1 teaspoon of cornflour and mix well again.

Heat a wok or frying pan to a high heat. Add 1 tablespoon of vegetable oil and spread the egg noodles out over the pan. Reduce the heat to low and cook for 3–4 minutes. Flip the noodle nest, add another tablespoon of vegetable oil and fry for a further 3–4 minutes. Remove the noodles, drain any excess oil and arrange the nest in the bottom of a long foil tray.

Heat the wok or frying pan to a high heat once again. Add a little vegetable oil. Drop the chicken pieces into the pan and leave for 30 seconds to seal. Add the sliced onion and bean sprouts to the pan and stir-fry for around 3–4 minutes or until the chicken is just cooked through.

Add the prepared sauce to the pan and cook for a further minute or until the sauce just begins to thicken.

Pour the chicken and sauce on top of the noodle nest and place a lid on the container. Set aside to stand for 5–10 minutes and serve.

CHICKEN IN BLACK PEPPER SAUCE

(CHINESE TAKEAWAY STYLE)

Serves 1

This dish is made deliciously spicy with a combination of white and black pepper.

1 onion, chopped
½ red pepper, chopped
½ green pepper, chopped
3 tablespoons oyster sauce
½ teaspoon soy sauce (recommended brand: Kikkoman)
1 teaspoon black pepper
½ teaspoon white pepper
1 teaspoon sake
100 ml/3½ fl oz water or Chinese stock (page 185)
1 large skinless, boneless chicken breast fillet (around 113 g/
    4 oz total weight)
¼ teaspoon soy sauce
¼ teaspoon garlic powder
Pinch of ginger powder
1 teaspoon vegetable oil plus extra for frying
1 teaspoon cornflour
1 finger chilli pepper, finely sliced (optional, see page 62)

In a small bowl, combine the onion, red pepper and green pepper. Set aside.

In a separate small bowl, combine the oyster sauce, soy sauce, black pepper, white pepper, sake and water or Chinese stock. Mix well and set aside.

Trim any excess fat from the chicken breast and cut into small bite sized pieces. Add the soy sauce, garlic powder, ginger powder and vegetable oil. Mix well and marinade for 5 minutes. Add 1 teaspoon of cornflour and mix well again.

Heat a wok or frying pan to a high heat. Add a little vegetable oil. Drop the chicken pieces into the pan and leave for 30 seconds to seal. Stir-fry the chicken for around 3–4 minutes or until just cooked through. Remove and set aside.

Add the onion, red pepper and green pepper to the pan. Add another touch of oil if the pan becomes too dry. Reduce the heat to medium and stir-fry the vegetables for 3–4 minutes or until slightly charred and just beginning to soften.

Return the chicken to the pan and pour in the prepared black pepper sauce. Mix well and cook for a further 3–4 minutes on a medium-high heat, stirring occasionally until the sauce is thick, syrupy and well reduced.

Pour the chicken and sauce into a long foil tray and garnish with finely sliced chilli if desired. Serve with egg fried rice and prawn crackers.

KUNG PAO CHICKEN
(Chinese Takeaway Style)

Serves 1

¼ red pepper, chopped
¼ green pepper, chopped
½ small onion, chopped
1 dried red chilli pepper
Dash of dry sherry
1 teaspoon rice wine vinegar
1 tablespoon soy sauce (recommended brand: Kikkoman)
½ teaspoon toasted sesame oil
1 teaspoon sugar
2 tablespoons Chinese stock (page 185) or water
½ teaspoon cornflour
1 large chicken breast (around 113 g/4 oz total weight)
½ teaspoon soy sauce (recommended brand: Kikkoman)
1 tablespoon vegetable oil plus extra for frying
½ teaspoon cornflour
2 teaspoons garlic and ginger paste (page 182)
2 tablespoons roasted peanuts

In a small bowl, combine the red pepper, green pepper, onion and dried red chilli pepper. Set aside.

In a separate small bowl, combine the dry sherry, rice wine vinegar, soy sauce, toasted sesame oil, sugar, Chinese stock or water and cornflour.

Trim any excess fat from the chicken breast and cut into small pieces. Add the ½ teaspoon of soy sauce and vegetable oil. Mix well and add the ½ teaspoon of cornflour. Mix well again.

Heat a wok or frying pan to a high heat. Add a little vegetable oil. Drop the chicken pieces into the pan and leave for 30 seconds to seal. Stir-fry the chicken for around 3–4 minutes or until just cooked through. Remove and set aside.

Add the prepared vegetables to the pan. Add another touch of oil if the pan becomes too dry. Reduce the heat to medium and stir-fry the vegetables for 2 minutes.

Add the garlic and ginger paste and mix well. Stir-fry for 1 minute.

Return the chicken to the pan and pour in the prepared kung pao sauce. Mix well and cook for a further minute or until the sauce begins to thicken. Add the roasted peanuts and mix well.

Pour the kung pao chicken into a long foil tray and serve with egg fried rice or plain chow mein.

BREAST OF CHICKEN PEKING STYLE
(CHINESE TAKEAWAY STYLE)

Serves 1

Coleman's OK sauce is similar to traditional brown sauce but with a more distinct fruity note. Most Chinese supermarkets will stock this sauce, however if it cannot be sourced then traditional HP brown sauce will make an adequate replacement.

½ red pepper, chopped
½ green pepper, chopped
1 small onion, chopped
2 tablespoons Worcester sauce
3 tablespoons tomato ketchup
1 tablespoon Coleman's OK sauce (or brown sauce)
1 teaspoon sweet chilli sauce (page 183)
2 teaspoons soy sauce (recommended brand: Kikkoman)
1 teaspoon rice wine vinegar
¼ teaspoon white sugar
Large pinch of Chinese 5-spice
8 tablespoons water
1 large skinless, boneless chicken breast fillet (around 113 g/
    4 oz weight)
¼ teaspoon soy sauce (recommended brand: Kikkoman)
¼ teaspoon garlic powder
Pinch of ginger powder
1 teaspoon vegetable oil plus extra for frying
1 teaspoon cornflour

In a small bowl, combine the red pepper, green pepper and onion. Set aside.

In a large bowl, combine the Worcester sauce, tomato ketchup, OK or brown sauce, sweet chilli sauce, soy sauce, rice wine vinegar, white sugar, Chinese 5-spice and water. Mix thoroughly and set aside.

Trim any excess fat from the chicken breast and cut into bite-sized pieces. Add the soy sauce, garlic powder, ginger powder and vegetable oil. Mix well and marinade for 5 minutes. Add 1 teaspoon of cornflour and mix well again.

Heat a wok or frying pan to a high heat. Add a little vegetable oil. Drop the chicken pieces into the pan and leave for 30 seconds to seal. Stir-fry the chicken for around 3–4 minutes or until just cooked through. Remove and set aside.

Add the prepared vegetables to the pan. Add another touch of oil if the pan becomes too dry. Stir-fry for 2–3 minutes.

Return the chicken to the pan and pour in the prepared Peking sauce. Mix well and cook for a further 1–2 minutes or until the sauce just begins to thicken. Serve with egg fried rice or plain chow mein.

CHICKEN MUSHROOM

(CHINESE TAKEAWAY STYLE)

Serves 1

Preparing this dish in the same way as your local Chinese takeaway requires deep-frying of the mushrooms, ensuring that they remain juicy on the inside. This can be done in a small pan filled one-third full with oil. Alternatively, the mushrooms may be fried alongside the chicken with acceptable results.

6 tablespoons Chinese stock (page 185) or water
2 teaspoons oyster sauce
Pinch of black pepper
Pinch of white pepper
1 large skinless, boneless chicken breast fillet (around 113 g/ 4 oz weight)
½ teaspoon soy sauce (recommended brand: Kikkoman)
½ teaspoon garlic powder
Pinch of ginger powder
1 tablespoon vegetable oil
1 teaspoon cornflour
Oil for deep frying
6 button mushrooms, halved
1 medium onion, chopped
½ teaspoon soy sauce (recommended brand: Kikkoman)
Pinch of salt
2 teaspoons cornflour mixed with 4 teaspoons water

In a small bowl, combine the Chinese stock or water, oyster sauce, black pepper and white pepper. Set aside.

Trim any excess fat from the chicken breast and cut into bite sized pieces. Add the soy sauce, garlic powder, ginger powder and vegetable oil. Mix well and marinade for 5 minutes. Add 1 teaspoon of cornflour and mix well again.

Heat a wok or frying pan to a high heat. Add a little vegetable oil. Drop the chicken pieces into the wok and leave for 30 seconds to seal. Stir-fry the chicken for around 3–4 minutes or until just cooked through. Remove and set aside.

Heat oil for deep-frying over a medium heat. When the oil is hot, deep-fry the mushrooms for 20–30 seconds. Remove the mushrooms from the pan, drain off any excess oil and place in the wok used to fry the chicken.

Add the chopped onion to the wok with the mushrooms and stir-fry over a high heat for 1 minute. Return the chicken to the wok and add ½ teaspoon of soy sauce and a pinch of salt. Mix well and stir-fry for a further 1–2 minutes.

Add the prepared sauce to the wok, reduce the heat slightly and stir-fry for 30 seconds. Add the prepared cornflour and water mixture and cook for a further 2 minutes on a low heat until the sauce thickens slightly.

Serve with egg fried rice or plain chow mein.

SWEET AND SOUR PORK
HONG KONG STYLE

(CHINESE TAKEAWAY STYLE)

Serves 1

¼ red pepper, chopped
¼ green pepper, chopped
¼ yellow pepper, chopped
½ onion, chopped
1 tinned pineapple ring, chopped
75 ml/2½ fl oz rice wine vinegar
100 ml/3½ fl oz water
2 tablespoons tomato ketchup
1 tablespoon white sugar
1 tablespoon brown sugar
½ teaspoon soy sauce
1 large pork loin steak (around 113 g/4 oz weight)
Pinch of salt and pinch of black pepper
1 egg
6 tablespoons cornflour
Vegetable oil for deep frying
1 teaspoon of cornflour mixed with 2 tablespoons of water

In a bowl, combine the red pepper, green pepper, yellow pepper, onion and pineapple. Set aside.

In a small pot, combine the rice wine vinegar, water, tomato ketchup, white sugar, brown sugar and soy sauce. Bring to the boil, reduce the heat to low and simmer for 2 minutes or until the sugar is dissolved. Set aside.

Trim any excess fat from the pork loin steak and cut into small bite sized pieces. Add the salt and pepper and mix well.

Whisk the egg in a bowl and add the seasoned pork pieces. Mix thoroughly. Add the 6 tablespoons of cornflour to a separate bowl.

Lift the pork pieces out of the egg mixture, discarding any excess egg. Place the pork pieces into the bowl with the cornflour and toss well until each piece is fully coated. Place the coated pork pieces onto a baking tray in a single layer in order to ensure they don't stick together.

Heat the oil for deep-frying to a medium-high heat. Carefully drop the pork pieces into the pan and fry for 3–4 minutes until crispy and just cooked through. Remove the pork from the pan, drain off any excess oil and set aside.

Heat a wok or frying pan to a high heat. Add a little vegetable oil. Pour the prepared bowl of vegetables into the pan and stir-fry for 2–3 minutes.

Reduce the heat to low and add the sweet and sour sauce. Cook for 20 seconds then stir the cornflour/water mixture and slowly add to the pan, stirring until the sauce thickens slightly.

Add the cooked pork pieces and mix thoroughly. Serve with egg fried rice or plain chow mein.

CRISPY BEEF WITH SWEET CHILLI SAUCE

(CHINESE TAKEAWAY STYLE)

Serves 1

1 small onion, sliced
½ carrot, peeled into thin strips
1 spring onion, cut into 3 pieces
1 red finger chilli pepper, sliced (optional, see page 62)
2 tablespoons sweet chilli sauce (page 183)
2 tablespoons water
2 tablespoons rice wine vinegar
¼ teaspoon sugar
½ teaspoon soy sauce (recommended brand: Kikkoman)
1 x 200 g/7 oz sirloin steak
Pinch of salt
Pinch of black pepper
1 egg
8 tablespoons cornflour
Oil for deep frying

In a small bowl, combine the onion, carrot and spring onion. Add the red chilli pepper if desired. Set aside.

In a separate small bowl, combine the sweet chilli sauce, water, rice wine vinegar, sugar and soy sauce. Set aside.

Trim any excess fat from the steak and slice into extremely thin strips. Add the salt and pepper and mix well.

Whisk the egg in a large bowl. Place the cornflour in a separate large bowl.

Drop the steak slices into the whisked egg. Mix well. Lift the steak slices out of the bowl with your hands, allowing excess egg to drain back into the bowl.

Drop the egg coated steak slices into the bowl of cornflour and mix well. The steak slices should become completely dry and fully coated in flour. Add more cornflour if necessary.

Heat the oil for deep-frying over a medium-high heat. Carefully drop the flour coated steak strips into the oil and fry for around 8 minutes or until crisp.

Heat a wok or frying pan to a high heat. Add a little vegetable oil. Add the prepared vegetables and stir-fry for 1–2 minutes. Add 1 tablespoon of water as the pan becomes dry. The water will evaporate and steam will help to soften the vegetables slightly.

Reduce the heat to medium-low and add the prepared sauce mixture. Mix well and cook for 20–30 seconds or until the sauce becomes slightly thick.

Drain any excess oil from the crispy beef and add it to the wok with the vegetables and sauce. Mix well until the beef is coated in sauce. Pour the crispy beef into a long foil tray and serve with egg fried rice or plain chow mein.

MONGOLIAN BEEF

(Chinese Takeaway Style)

Serves 1

2 tablespoons hoisin sauce
2 teaspoons soy sauce (recommended brand: Kikkoman)
4 tablespoons Chinese stock (page 185) or water
2 garlic cloves, crushed
¼ red pepper, finely sliced
2 mild chilli peppers, sliced (see page 62)
4 spring onions, each cut into 4 pieces
1 x 200 g/7 oz sirloin steak
1 tablespoon dry sherry
1 teaspoon cornflour
2 tablespoons vegetable oil

In a small bowl, combine the hoisin sauce, soy sauce and Chinese stock or water. Mix well. Set aside.

In a separate small bowl, combine the garlic, red pepper, chilli peppers and spring onions. Set aside.

Trim any excess fat from the steak and slice into thin pieces. Add the dry sherry and cornflour and mix well. Set aside for 5 minutes.

Heat the 2 tablespoons of vegetable oil in a wok or frying pan over a high heat. Add the steak slices and leave for 30 seconds to seal. Stir-fry for 2–3 minutes or until just cooked through. Remove the steak slices from the pan and set aside.

Wipe the pan clean and add a touch more vegetable oil. Add the prepared vegetables and stir-fry for 1–2 minutes. Return the steak pieces to the pan and mix well. Stir-fry for a further 30 seconds.

Add the prepared sauce and mix well. Cook for a further 2 minutes or until the sauce begins to thicken.

Pour the Mongolian beef into a long foil tray and serve with egg fried rice or plain chow mein.

MIXED VEGETABLE CHOP SUEY

(CHINESE TAKEAWAY STYLE)

Serves 1

Chop Suey literally translates as 'assorted pieces', hence the assortment of mixed vegetables included in the dish.

1 onion, chopped
½ red pepper, chopped
½ green pepper, chopped
3–4 broccoli florets, steamed for 3–4 minutes and cooled
3 button mushrooms, sliced
1 small handful shredded pak choi or green cabbage
1 small handful bean sprouts
5–6 tablespoons light vegetable stock or water
1 tablespoon oyster sauce
1 teaspoon soy sauce
1 teaspoon dry sherry
¼ teaspoon white sugar
Small pinch of black pepper
Small pinch of white pepper
1 tablespoon vegetable oil

In a large bowl, combine the onion, red pepper, green pepper, steamed broccoli, mushrooms, shredded pak choi or green cabbage and bean sprouts. Set aside.

In a small bowl, combine the vegetable stock or water, oyster sauce, soy sauce, dry sherry, white sugar, black pepper and white pepper. Mix thoroughly.

Heat a wok or frying pan over a high heat. Add the tablespoon of vegetable oil. Add the prepared vegetables and stir-fry for 3–4 minutes.

Add the prepared sauce and mix well. Cook for a further 2 minutes or until the sauce is slightly reduced.

Serve with plain chow mein or egg fried rice.

SPECIAL FRIED RICE

(Chinese Takeaway Style)

Serves 1

This dish can be created from scratch or made up of any variety of cooked meats. Save leftover chicken, pork and prawns from Chinese dishes and freeze for up to 1 month. When enough meat is collected, defrost and reheat thoroughly using this recipe.

1 egg
½ teaspoon toasted sesame oil
1 portion precooked rice (page 188)
Pinch of salt
1 teaspoon soy sauce (recommended brand: Kikkoman) OR ½
    teaspoon each of light and dark soy sauce
2 tablespoons frozen mixed vegetables, heated in the
    microwave or boiled according to instructions
1 small handful of cooked Chinese chicken, shredded
1 small handful of cooked Chinese roast pork, shredded OR 2
    slices lean bacon, cooked and chopped
4 large cooked king prawns
1 tablespoon oyster sauce
½ teaspoon soy sauce (recommended brand: Kikkoman)
2 tablespoons Chinese stock (page 185) or water

In a small bowl, combine the egg and toasted sesame oil. Whisk thoroughly.

Heat a little vegetable oil in a wok over a high heat. Add the egg mixture and tilt the pan. Break up the egg into small pieces with a spatula and stir-fry for 1–2 minutes or until the egg is cooked. Remove and set aside.

Add a touch more oil to the pan and return to a medium-high heat. Add the cooked rice and stir-fry immediately to ensure all of the rice is coated in oil. Add the salt and stir-fry for 3–4 minutes or until the rice is dry and thoroughly reheated. Add the soy sauce and mix again until the rice is evenly coloured. Pour the rice into a long foil tray. Cover loosely with a lid to keep warm.

Add a final touch of vegetable oil to the pan over a high heat. Add the heated mixed vegetables, chicken, roast pork or bacon and king prawns. Stir-fry for a further 2–3 minutes or until the meat is thoroughly reheated.

Add the oyster sauce, soy sauce and Chinese stock or water. Mix well once again and cook for a further minute over a high heat. Pour the meat and vegetables over the fried rice and serve.

MUSHROOM OMELETTE
(Chinese Takeaway Style)

Serves 1

A well seasoned or non-stick wok helps greatly in making omelettes and is well worth investing in.

4 small button mushrooms, sliced
2 eggs
½ teaspoon toasted sesame oil
1 tablespoon vegetable oil
¼ teaspoon salt

Heat a little vegetable oil in the wok over a high heat. Add the sliced mushrooms and stir-fry for 2–3 minutes or until cooked. Remove and set aside.

In a small bowl, combine the eggs and toasted sesame oil. Whisk thoroughly.

Add the tablespoon of vegetable oil to the wok over a high heat. Reduce the heat to medium and pour the egg mixture into the wok. Add the cooked mushrooms and tilt the pan to ensure uncooked egg runs to the side of the pan.

Shake the pan around in a circular motion. Use a ladle to hold the mushroom and cooked egg mixture in the middle of the pan and tilt the pan once again. Any uncooked egg mixture will again run to the side of the pan.

Continue to shake the pan in a circular motion so that the egg stays together. Season with salt and increase the heat to medium-high. Using one swift motion, flip the omelette over in the pan. This may take some practice and is made easier with a well-shaped wok and a high heat.

Press down on the omelette with the ladle in order to help the omelette brown evenly. Flip the egg again a few times until completely cooked. The omelette should cook within 2–3 minutes.

Fold the mushroom omelette into a long foil tray and serve.

6

INDIAN

Indian curry remains one of the most popular takeaway foods and thankfully more and more restaurants are now adding a broader selection of dishes to the menu. A whole host of curries are on offer today, providing a dish for every taste, including those of us who may not enjoy overly spicy foods.

While it's true that most British Indian curries bear little resemblance to authentic and traditional Indian dishes, the quality and diversity remains. Although sharing many ingredients, the specific preparation style of each dish results in a vast array of flavours.

Many Indian restaurants cook with butter ghee, a clarified butter that is rich in flavour. This can be found in large supermarkets. However, vegetable oil is an acceptable (and healthier) alternative. While many of the dishes in this chapter rely heavily on oil content, a properly cooked curry should show oil separation in the pan and so excess oil can be removed if desired. Although this is an option, the curry dishes themselves should be cooked with the amount of oil listed in the ingredients and removed after cooking. Cooking with less oil will result in the spices being undercooked and will have a negative effect on the flavour of the curry.

The oil content is of course an acceptable trade-off when accompanied by the long list of lean meats, vegetables and spices included in the various dishes on offer. Turmeric is often said to have excellent anti-inflammatory properties and research is ongoing into the many health benefits it (and other spices) may offer. Of course, garlic is said to help keep your heart healthy and so the combination of ingredients in curry dishes can happily become a regular and healthy addition to your diet.

The use of food colourings is the cause of much debate where Indian takeaway dishes are concerned. The recipes included in this chapter do not call for the use of any food colourings. Should you wish to use them in your Indian cooking, there is a wide variety of natural food colourings available today which are much more highly recommended from a health point of view than their artificial alternatives. Regardless of whether the colourings used are natural or artificial, they will add only colour, not flavour. Colour can also be added to your dishes using healthy spices such as turmeric and paprika.

Frozen food products are frequently used to help make life easy for restaurant chefs (and now the home cook). Many supermarkets sell a frozen vegetable mixture containing broccoli, cauliflower, peas and carrots. These frozen mixes are inexpensive and perfect for use in curries or rice dishes.

Garlic and ginger paste is commonly made fresh by restaurants as the flavour it brings to each curry dish is far superior to that found in shop bought pastes. These can be used if desired however. If only individual pastes are available, you can make your own combination by combining 3 parts garlic paste to 1 part ginger paste.

The curry recipes in this chapter may be adjusted slightly if a hotter or milder curry is desired. If the dish will be shared among people with different tastes, fresh chilli peppers may be added whole and served to those who are brave enough! However, be careful when preparing them, as they can cause a burning sensation when in contact with the skin. Wash your hands thoroughly after touching them.

Store cupboard ingredients widely used in Indian curry dishes include:

Cumin powder
Coriander powder
Turmeric powder
Paprika powder
Garam masala powder
Mild Madras curry powder
Chilli powder

Dried fenugreek leaves (also known as methi leaves)
Tomato purée
Tinned tomatoes
Chapati flour
Gram flour (also known as chickpea flour)
Vegetable oil or ghee

SAVOURY BASIC CURRY SAUCE

(INDIAN RESTAURANT STYLE)

Makes enough sauce for 6–8 curries

This smooth take on the 'base gravy' used in many Indian restaurants has a strong flavour all of its own, perfectly matched with the curry dishes included in this chapter.

150 ml/5 fl oz vegetable oil
3 large Spanish onions (around 800 g/2 lb peeled weight), chopped
1 large carrot, peeled and chopped
½ green pepper, chopped
½ red pepper, chopped
2 finger chilli peppers, chopped (see page 62)
1 large handful fresh coriander leaves and stalks, finely chopped
1 small baby/new potato, peeled
2 tablespoons garlic and ginger paste (page 182)
1 teaspoon salt
2.5 litres/4½ pints water
3–4 green cardamom pods (optional)
200 g/7 oz tinned chopped tomatoes (½ an average tin)
2 generous tablespoons restaurant spice mix (page 181)

In a large pot, add the vegetable oil, onions, carrot, green pepper, red pepper, chilli peppers, fresh coriander, potato, garlic and ginger paste, salt and water. Add the cardamom pods if desired.

Bring to a boil, cover with a lid and set the heat to medium–high. Boil the vegetables for 30 minutes.

Add the chopped tomatoes and spice mix. Mix thoroughly.

Reduce the heat to medium–low and cook for a further 20 minutes. Allow the sauce to cool slightly then blend with a hand blender until completely smooth. Add more water (around 1 litre/1¾ pints) while blending until the curry sauce has the consistency of a thin soup.

The prepared basic curry sauce will keep well in the fridge for up to 3 days or can be frozen in 300 ml/10½ fl oz batches for use in any curry dish.

CHICKEN MADRAS
(INDIAN RESTAURANT STYLE)

Serves 1–2

Hot and spicy, with a generous amount of rich curry sauce.

300 ml/10½ fl oz savoury basic curry sauce (page 63)
2 tablespoons vegetable oil
½ teaspoon garlic and ginger paste (page 182)
Pinch of salt
1 tablespoon tomato purée, mixed with 2 tablespoons water
1 teaspoon dried fenugreek leaves
1 tablespoon restaurant spice mix (page 181)
1 tablespoon chilli powder
1 portion precooked curry chicken (page 187)
1 teaspoon lemon juice
1 small handful fresh coriander, finely chopped

In a small pan, bring the savoury basic curry sauce to boiling point. Stir well, switch off the heat and set aside.

Heat the vegetable oil in a frying pan or wok over a medium heat. Add the garlic and ginger paste, salt, tomato purée and water mixture, dried fenugreek leaves, restaurant spice mix and chilli powder. Stir-fry for around 30 seconds, adding a little basic curry sauce to ensure the spices do not burn if the pan becomes too dry.

Add around half (150 ml/5 fl oz) of the basic curry sauce and mix again. Stir-fry over a medium heat for 3–4 minutes

Add the precooked chicken and lemon juice and mix well. Add the remaining base and mix thoroughly. Add the fresh coriander and continue to cook over a medium–high heat for a further 3–4 minutes or until the sauce reaches the desired consistency.

Pour the chicken Madras into a long foil tray and garnish with a little extra coriander. Serve with tava chapatis (page 118) and Indian fried rice (page 126).

MILD INDIAN CURRY SAUCE

(INDIAN RESTAURANT STYLE)

Serves 1–2

300 ml/10½ fl oz savoury basic curry sauce (page 63)
2 tablespoons vegetable oil
½ small onion, sliced
¼ green pepper, finely sliced
¼ red pepper, finely sliced
1 teaspoon garlic and ginger paste (page 182)
2 tablespoons tomato purée mixed with 4 tablespoons water
Pinch of salt
½ teaspoon dried fenugreek leaves
1 tablespoon restaurant spice mix (page 181)

In a small pan, bring the savoury basic curry sauce to boiling point. Stir well, switch off the heat and set aside.

Heat the oil over a medium heat. Add the onion, green and red pepper and stir-fry for 2–3 minutes. Add the garlic and ginger paste and stir-fry for a further 30 seconds.

Add the tomato purée and water mixture, salt, dried fenugreek and restaurant spice mix. Stir-fry for 30 seconds, adding a little basic curry sauce if the pan becomes too dry.

Add around half (150 ml/5 fl oz) of the savoury basic curry sauce and mix well. Increase the heat to medium-high and stir-fry for around 3–4 minutes.

Add the remaining basic curry sauce and mix thoroughly once again. Continue to cook over a medium-high heat for a further 3–4 minutes or until the sauce reaches the desired consistency.

Pour the curry sauce into a foil tray and garnish with fresh coriander. Serve with chicken biryani (page 68).

NORTH INDIAN GARLIC CHILLI CHICKEN

(INDIAN RESTAURANT STYLE)

Serves 1–2

Sweet, hot and spicy, this colourful curry dish is packed full of flavour. Although any good quality sweet chilli sauce may be used, it's worth the extra effort to prepare the one included in this book (page 183).

200 ml/7 fl oz savoury basic curry sauce (page 63)
2 tablespoons vegetable oil
¼ green pepper, finely chopped
4 garlic cloves, finely sliced
1 tablespoon garlic and ginger paste (page 182)
1 green finger chilli pepper, chopped (see page 62)
1 tablespoon tomato purée, mixed with 2 tablespoons of water
½ tin peeled plum tomatoes, blended (around 200 g/7 oz)
1 tablespoon restaurant spice mix (page 181)
¼ teaspoon paprika
2 teaspoons dried fenugreek leaves
½ teaspoon sugar
Pinch of salt
1 spring onion, finely sliced
1 tablespoon sweet chilli sauce (page 183)
1 portion precooked curry chicken (page 187)
1 small handful fresh coriander leaves, finely chopped

In a small pan, bring the basic curry sauce to boiling point. Stir well, switch off the heat and set aside.

Heat the vegetable oil in a frying pan or wok over a medium heat. Add the green pepper, garlic cloves, garlic and ginger paste and chilli pepper. Mix well and stir-fry for 1 minute.

Add the tomato purée and water mixture, blended plum tomatoes, restaurant spice mix, paprika, dried fenugreek leaves, sugar, salt, spring onion and sweet chilli sauce. Mix well and stir-fry for 2 minutes.

Add around half (100 ml/3½ fl oz) of the savoury basic curry sauce and mix well. Add the precooked curry chicken, increase the heat to medium-high and stir-fry for around 3–4 minutes.

Add the remaining basic curry sauce and mix thoroughly once again. Continue to cook over a medium-high heat for a further 3–4 minutes or until the sauce reaches the desired consistency.

Pour the curry into a long foil tray and garnish with fresh coriander. Serve with Indian fried rice (page 126).

CHICKEN BIRYANI WITH MILD CURRY SAUCE

(INDIAN RESTAURANT STYLE)

Serves 1–2

2 tablespoons vegetable oil
½ small onion, finely chopped
Pinch of salt
1 teaspoon dried fenugreek leaves
1 tablespoon almonds
1 tablespoon raisins
1 tablespoon sultanas
1 portion precooked curry chicken (page 187), shredded
1 tablespoon restaurant spice mix (page 181)
1 portion precooked rice (page 188)
3–4 thin tomato slices
3–4 thin slices of cucumber
1 tablespoon fresh coriander, finely chopped

Heat the vegetable oil in a wok or frying pan over a medium heat. Add the chopped onion, salt, dried fenugreek, almonds, raisins, sultanas and precooked chicken.

Mix well and stir-fry for 2–3 minutes. Add the restaurant spice mix and stir-fry for 30–40 seconds.

Add the precooked rice and mix well. Stir-fry for 2–3 minutes or until the rice is hot.

Pour the chicken biryani into a long foil tray and top with tomato, cucumber and fresh coriander.

Serve with mild Indian curry sauce (page 65).

PUNJABI CHICKEN KORMA

(INDIAN RESTAURANT STYLE)

Serves 1–2

This variation on the traditional korma uses almond powder and less sugar to provide a balanced flavour.

300 ml/10 ½ fl oz savoury basic curry sauce (page 63)
2 tablespoons vegetable oil
3 generous tablespoons coconut flour
1 tablespoon sugar
2 generous tablespoons almond powder
5–6 raisins
1 portion precooked curry chicken (page 187)
3–4 tablespoons single cream

In a small pan, bring the savoury basic curry sauce to boiling point. Stir well, switch off the heat and set aside.

Heat the oil over a medium heat. Add the coconut flour, sugar and almond powder. Mix thoroughly.

Add the raisins and precooked curry chicken. Mix well once more.

Add the prepared basic curry sauce. Increase the heat to medium-high and cook for 5–6 minutes or until the sauce begins to thicken and reaches the desired consistency. Stir the sauce occasionally.

Add the single cream to the curry sauce. Mix well, switch off the heat and pour the curry into a long foil tray.

Serve with poppadoms and tava chapatis (page 118).

SPICY CHICKEN PURI

(INDIAN RESTAURANT STYLE)

Serves 1–2

This Indian starter dish is perfect when time is short as it doesn't rely on basic curry sauce and can be cooked in around 15 minutes.

2 cooked puri breads (page 117)
2 tablespoons onion salad (page 125)
1 portion precooked curry chicken (page 187)
1 tablespoon vegetable oil
½ small onion, finely chopped
¼ teaspoon garlic and ginger paste (page 182)
1 teaspoon tomato purée mixed with 1 tablespoon water
1 teaspoon mild curry paste (recommended brand: Patak's)
1 teaspoon restaurant spice mix (page 181)
Pinch of chilli powder
¼ teaspoon salt
1 teaspoon dried fenugreek leaves
200 g/7 oz tinned chopped tomatoes (around ½ a tin)
Around 150 ml/5 fl oz water
½ teaspoon coconut powder or sugar (optional)
½ fresh tomato, sliced
1 small handful of coriander, finely chopped
½ lemon, sliced to serve

In a large serving tray, arrange the cooked puri breads. Arrange the onion salad in one corner of the tray.

Cut the precooked chicken into small cubes. Set aside.

Heat the vegetable oil in a frying pan or wok over a medium heat. Add the chopped onion and garlic and ginger paste. Stir-fry for 1–2 minutes.

Add the tomato purée/water mixture, curry paste, restaurant spice mix, chilli powder, salt and dried fenugreek leaves. Stir-fry for 1 minute.

Add the tinned tomatoes and water. Add the coconut powder or sugar if desired. Add the cooked chicken pieces. Mix well and turn the heat up to medium-high.

Stir-fry for 2–3 minutes. Add the fresh tomato slices and fresh coriander.

Stir-fry for a further 2–3 minutes. If the pan becomes too dry, add a little more tinned tomato or water. The finished dish should be thick with very little sauce.

Pour the chicken pieces and sauce over the puri breads. Garnish with a little extra fresh coriander. Serve with lemon slices.

STAFF CURRY

(INDIAN RESTAURANT STYLE)

Serves 2–3

Originally created to help keep busy restaurant staff going during a busy shift, slow cooked staff curry is now a hugely popular menu item.

1 tablespoon coriander powder
1 tablespoon cumin powder
½ teaspoon turmeric
½ teaspoon chilli powder
½ teaspoon salt
2 tablespoons vegetable oil
2 medium onions, finely chopped
1 tablespoon garlic and ginger paste (page 182)
1 tablespoon tomato purée
500 g/1.1 lb braising steak, diced
½ tin peeled plum tomatoes (around 200 g/7 oz)
500 ml/18 fl oz water
5–6 small baby potatoes
1 teaspoon garam masala
1 teaspoon lemon juice

In a small bowl, combine the coriander powder, cumin powder, turmeric, chilli powder and salt. Set aside.

In a large pot, heat the vegetable oil over a low heat. Add the chopped onions and stir-fry for 5–6 minutes until soft and golden.

Add the garlic and ginger paste and tomato purée. Stir-fry for 30 seconds.

Add the prepared spice mix. Stir-fry over a medium-low heat for 2 minutes, adding a little juice from the plum tomatoes if the mixture becomes too dry.

Add the braising steak and increase the heat to medium-high. Fry the mixture for 2 minutes or until the steak pieces are sealed.

Add the tinned tomatoes and water. Bring to the boil and mix well.

Place a lid on the pan and reduce the heat to low. Simmer for around 1½ hours or until the liquid is reduced and slightly thickened.

Add the baby potatoes and simmer for a further 30–40 minutes or until the potatoes are soft.

Add the garam masala and lemon juice. Simmer for a further 2 minutes.

Switch off the heat and allow the curry to settle for 5 minutes. Serve with rice and tava chapati breads (page 118).

Leftover Staff Curry will freeze well for up to 1 month.

CHICKPEA AND MUSHROOM DOPIAZA

(INDIAN RESTAURANT STYLE)

Serves 1–2

Dopiaza literally translates as 'double onion', hence the use of 1 whole onion combined with an already onion-rich savoury curry sauce.

1 pinch of coriander seeds
1 pinch of cumin seeds
350 ml/12 fl oz savoury basic curry sauce (page 63)
2 tablespoons vegetable oil
½ green pepper, sliced
1 medium onion, sliced
6 tablespoons frozen mixed vegetables (broccoli, cauliflower, carrots, peas)
1 heaped teaspoon garlic and ginger paste (page 182)
1 tablespoon tomato purée, mixed with 1 tablespoon water
1 tablespoon tomato ketchup
1½ tablespoons restaurant spice mix (page 181)
Pinch of salt
1 teaspoon dried fenugreek leaves
½ tin chickpeas (around 200 g/7 oz), rinsed and drained
6 small button mushrooms
1 small handful fresh coriander leaves, finely chopped

Crush the coriander and cumin seeds in a pestle and mortar, or with the back of a spoon. Set aside in a small bowl.

In a small pot, bring the savoury basic curry sauce to boiling point. Stir well, switch off the heat and set aside.

Heat the vegetable oil in a frying pan or wok over a low-medium heat. Add the green pepper, onion and frozen mixed vegetables. Stir-fry for 2–3 minutes.

Add the garlic and ginger paste and stir-fry for a further 30 seconds. Add the tomato purée and water mixture, tomato ketchup, restaurant spice mix, salt and dried fenugreek leaves. Mix well and stir-fry for 30 seconds, adding a little basic curry sauce if the pan becomes too dry.

Add around half (175 ml/6 fl oz) of the savoury basic curry sauce. Add the chickpeas and button mushrooms. Mix thoroughly, increase the heat to medium-high and cook for 3–4 minutes.

Add the remaining basic curry sauce, mix well once again and continue to stir-fry for a further 3–4 minutes or until the sauce reaches the desired consistency.

Pour the curry into a long foil tray. Garnish with fresh coriander leaves and sprinkle over the prepared crushed coriander and cumin seed mixture. Serve with Indian fried rice (page 126).

MIXED VEGETABLE BALTI

(INDIAN RESTAURANT STYLE)

Serves 1–2

Traditionally a rich dish made with garlic, ginger, onion, peppers and a touch of mixed pickle.

5 baby potatoes, quartered
2–3 tablespoons frozen peas
6–8 medium frozen cauliflower florets
300 ml/10½ fl oz savoury basic curry sauce (page 63)
3 tablespoons vegetable oil
1 teaspoon garlic and ginger paste (page 182)
1 small onion, sliced
½ green pepper, sliced
1 tablespoon tomato purée, mixed with 2 tablespoons water
1 tablespoon restaurant spice mix (page 181)
Pinch of salt
1 tablespoon balti paste (recommended brand: Patak's)
½ teaspoon mixed pickle (recommended brand: Patak's)
1 teaspoon dried fenugreek leaves
1 spring onion, finely sliced
1 small handful fresh coriander leaves, finely chopped

Bring a large pot of water to the boil. Add the potatoes and simmer for 8 minutes.

Add the frozen peas and cauliflower florets. Bring back to the boil and simmer for a further 4 minutes. Drain the vegetables and set aside to cool. The prepared vegetables will keep well in the fridge for up to 24 hours.

In a small pot, bring the savoury basic curry sauce to boiling point. Stir well, switch off the heat and set aside.

Heat the vegetable oil in a frying pan or wok over a low-medium heat. Add the garlic and ginger paste, onion and green pepper. Mix well and stir-fry for 2 minutes.

Add the tomato purée and water mixture, restaurant spice mix, salt, balti paste, mixed pickle, dried fenugreek leaves and spring onion. Mix well and fry for 30 seconds.

Add around half (150 ml/5 fl oz) of the savoury basic curry sauce and mix well. Increase the heat to medium–high and stir-fry for 3–4 minutes. Stir and scrape the pan frequently to ensure the spices do not burn.

Add the remaining basic curry sauce and mix thoroughly once again. Add the prepared vegetables and stir-fry for a further 3–4 minutes or until the sauce is well reduced and has reached the desired consistency.

Pour the balti into a long foil tray and garnish with fresh coriander. Serve with Indian fried rice (page 126) and paratha bread (page 115).

BOMBAY ALOO

(Indian Restaurant Style)

Serves 1–2

This dish makes great use of new baby potatoes. When plentiful and in season, many restaurants will buy in bulk, parboil the potatoes and freeze for use all year round in this dish. Parboiled new potatoes will keep well in the freezer for up to 2 months.

4–5 small new baby potatoes per portion
1 teaspoon restaurant spice mix (page 181)
Pinch of chilli powder
Large pinch of dried fenugreek leaves
¼ teaspoon salt
2 tablespoons vegetable oil
½ small onion, finely chopped
1 tablespoon tomato purée mixed with 2 tablespoons water
150 ml/5 fl oz savoury basic curry sauce (page 63)
½ fresh tomato, sliced
Finely chopped fresh coriander to serve

Fill a large pot with water. Add a pinch of salt. Place the potatoes into the pot and bring to the boil.

Once boiling, simmer for 5–6 minutes on a medium heat or until just slightly soft. Remove the potatoes from the pan, drain and set aside to cool. Slice each potato into two pieces. New potatoes may be boiled in bulk in this way, cooled and frozen in portions for future use.

In a small bowl, add the restaurant spice mix, chilli powder, fenugreek leaves and salt. Set aside.

Heat the vegetable oil in a pan over a medium-high heat. Add the chopped onion and stir-fry for 30 seconds.

Add the tomato purée/water mixture and the prepared bowl of spices. Mix thoroughly.

Add the potatoes to the pan and mix well once again. Stir-fry for 1 minute.

Add the savoury basic curry sauce and mix well once again. Reduce the heat to medium. Simmer for 3–4 minutes or until the sauce thickens and the potatoes are heated through, stirring occasionally.

Add the fresh tomato slices. Pour the Bombay potatoes into a foil container and garnish with fresh coriander. Serve with paratha bread (page 115).

KING PRAWN BHUNA

(INDIAN RESTAURANT STYLE)

Serves 1–2

Bhuna is classed as a 'dry dish' curry with the sauce thick and well reduced.

300 ml/10½ fl oz savoury basic curry sauce (page 63)
2 tablespoons vegetable oil
1 small onion, chopped
¼ green pepper, chopped
½ teaspoon garlic and ginger paste (page 182)
2 tablespoons tomato purée mixed with 4 tablespoons water
Pinch of salt
½ teaspoon dried fenugreek leaves
1 tablespoon restaurant spice mix (page 181)
8–10 large king prawns, cooked
1 tomato, quartered
1 small handful fresh coriander leaves, finely chopped

In a small pan, bring the basic curry sauce to boiling point. Stir well, switch off the heat and set aside.

Heat the vegetable oil in a frying pan or wok over a medium heat. Add the onion and green pepper. Mix well and stir-fry for 1 minute. Add the garlic and ginger paste and stir-fry for a further 30 seconds.

Add the tomato purée and water mixture, salt, dried fenugreek leaves and restaurant spice mix. Mix well and stir-fry for 2 minutes, adding a little basic curry sauce to the pan if the mix becomes too dry.

Add around half (150 ml/5 fl oz) of the savoury basic curry sauce and mix well. Increase the heat to medium-high and stir-fry for around 3–4 minutes.

Add the cooked king prawns. Add the remaining basic curry sauce and mix thoroughly once again. Continue to cook over a medium-high heat for a further 3–4 minutes or until the sauce reaches the desired consistency. The bhuna should be well reduced and the gravy very thick and the pan becoming dry.

Add the quartered tomato and mix well. Pour the curry into a long foil tray and garnish with fresh coriander. Serve with Indian fried rice (page 126) and tava chapatis (page 118).

KING PRAWN VINDALOO

(INDIAN RESTAURANT STYLE)

Serves 1–2

One of the hottest curry sauces on the menu; this dish is heavy on the chilli powder and should be eaten with caution!

2 small baby potatoes
300 ml/10½ fl oz savoury basic curry sauce (page 63)
2 tablespoons vegetable oil
1 teaspoon garlic and ginger paste (page 182)
2 tablespoons tomato purée mixed with 4 tablespoons water
Pinch of salt
2 teaspoons dried fenugreek leaves
1 tablespoon restaurant spice mix (page 181)
2 tablespoons chilli powder
1 teaspoon lemon juice or lemon dressing
8–10 large king prawns, cooked
1 small handful fresh coriander leaves, finely chopped

In a large pan, cover the potatoes with plenty of water. Bring to the boil and simmer for 8–10 minutes or until the potatoes are just beginning to soften. Drain the potatoes and set aside to cool.

In a small pan, bring the basic curry sauce to boiling point. Stir well, switch off the heat and set aside.

Heat the vegetable oil in a frying pan or wok over a medium heat. Add the garlic and ginger paste and stir-fry for 30 seconds.

Add the tomato purée and water mixture, salt, dried fenugreek leaves, restaurant spice mix and chilli powder. Mix well and stir-fry for 1 minute, adding a little basic curry sauce to the pan if the mix becomes too dry.

Add the basic curry sauce and mix well. Add the lemon juice or lemon dressing and mix well once again. Stir-fry for 2 minutes.

Add the cooked king prawns and the prepared potatoes and stir thoroughly once again. Continue to cook over a medium-high heat for a further 3–4 minutes or until the sauce reaches the desired consistency. The finished vindaloo should have a generous amount of sauce. Pour the curry into a long foil tray and garnish with fresh coriander. Serve with aloo paratha breads (page 116).

TANDOORI KING PRAWN

(INDIAN RESTAURANT STYLE)

Serves 1–2

120 ml/4 fl oz natural yogurt
1 tablespoon vegetable oil
1 teaspoon lemon juice
1 teaspoon garlic and ginger paste (page 182)
½ teaspoon salt
½ teaspoon cumin powder
½ teaspoon chilli powder
½ teaspoon garam masala
Pinch of turmeric
1 teaspoon dried fenugreek leaves
8–10 large raw king prawns

In a large bowl, combine the natural yogurt, vegetable oil, lemon juice, garlic and ginger paste, salt, cumin powder, chilli powder and garam masala, turmeric and dried fenugreek leaves. Mix thoroughly.

Add the king prawns to the marinade and mix gently by hand. Set aside for 10 minutes.

Preheat the oven to 240°C/475°F/Gas Mark 9.

Wipe off any excess marinade from the prawns and arrange them on a baking tray. Place the tray into the oven on the highest shelf and bake for around 6–8 minutes or until the prawns are cooked.

Serve the tandoori prawns with onion salad (page 125) and minted yogurt dip (page 147).

6

PIZZA

As we attempt to recreate our favourite takeaway dishes at home, often it's necessary to improvise with different cooking equipment due to the lack of professional ovens and burners in the home. Pizza offers perhaps the biggest challenge in this regard. Restaurants rely on expensive commercial pizza ovens to achieve extremely high heats (in some cases upward of 500°C!). This high heat ensures that the pizza can be cooked in just a few minutes and contributes to the texture of the pizza base becoming crisp and chewy.

While it's difficult to recreate this kind of heat in a home oven, with the use of the right tools available to us we can at least guarantee that our pizzas will very closely match the real thing in taste and texture. Every oven is different and so it's worth experimenting. Soon you'll discover the best oven shelf and cooking temperature for your oven.

In order to achieve a crisp crust on our pizzas, we can use two things. First a good quality pizza pan (or screen) is essential. These pans are designed with holes across the surface of the pan, helping moisture to escape and also ensuring that the high heat of the oven browns the base of the pizza crust.

The second essential item is a good quality pizza stone. This is extremely useful as it helps to conduct a high, dry heat, so that your crust browns evenly underneath. If a crispy crust is important to you, a pizza stone is highly recommended.

To preheat your pizza stone, place it in the oven at the highest possible heat and leave for 1 hour. Your pizza can be placed directly on the stone, or placed on the pizza tray/screen on top of the stone.

Restaurants often cook their pizzas in the pan and slide them onto the oven floor for the last few seconds of cooking in order to properly brown the crust. This process is known as 'decking the pizza' and can be done at home by sliding your pizza off its pan and directly onto the pizza stone for the last few minutes of cooking.

The crust and sauce recipes included in this chapter are based on those dishes offered by the most popular American fast-food pizza restaurants. Of course, any preferred toppings may be added to your pizza. Less is more however and it's always worth checking that your pizza isn't too laden with toppings as this will cause the base to become soggy. Vegetables should be sliced or chopped very small before adding to the pizza to ensure they cook quickly and adhere to the base as opposed to falling off with every bite! With just a small scattering of ingredients, your pizza will cook evenly with a golden, crispy crust.

Many restaurants now offer a serving of jalapeno peppers, ideal to spice up any pizza. If you'd like to serve your pizzas the same way, simply pat dry 2–3 tablespoons of jarred jalapeno peppers, finely chop and pour into a small dipping bowl.

MEDIUM CRUST PIZZA BASE

(AMERICAN FAST-FOOD STYLE)

Makes enough dough for 2 x 25 cm/10 inch pizza bases

Light, crisp, chewy pizza dough, imitating the fast-food variety in every
way at a fraction of the price.

300 g/10½ oz strong white bread flour
1 teaspoon salt
½ tablespoon white sugar
1 tablespoon vegetable oil
½ teaspoon active dried yeast
210 ml/7 fl oz water

In a large bowl, combine the bread flour, salt, white sugar, vegetable oil
and yeast. Mix well and slowly add the water until the dough comes
together.

Flour a work surface and pour the dough out. Knead thoroughly for 3–4
minutes until the dough becomes smooth. Shape the dough into a ball.

Rub the bowl with a little vegetable oil. Return the dough to the bowl
and cover with oiled cling film. Set aside for around 1 hour or until
doubled in size.

Knock the air out of the risen dough, divide into two pieces and knead
for a further minute. Shape the dough into balls again.

Place each dough ball into a small bowl. Cover with oiled cling film and
refrigerate for 2 hours.

The dough is now ready for use and, using a rolling pin, can be rolled
out to make the appropriate sized pizza base. Or the dough can be
frozen as is for up to 1 month.

SWEET PIZZA SAUCE

(AMERICAN FAST-FOOD STYLE)

Makes enough sauce for 2 x 25 cm/10 inch pizza bases

This recipe makes use of some very basic ingredients to create a sauce with just a little sweetness, similar to that used in some of the world's most famous pizza delivery restaurants.

250 ml/9 fl oz tomato passata
½ teaspoon vegetable oil
½ teaspoon salt
½ teaspoon white sugar
½ teaspoon garlic powder
½ teaspoon dried oregano
½ teaspoon dried Italian herbs

In a small pot, combine the tomato passata, vegetable oil, salt, white sugar, garlic powder, dried oregano and dried Italian herbs. Mix well over a low heat and simmer for 5–6 minutes or until the sauce becomes thick.

Remove from the heat. Cool completely and store in the refrigerator for up to 3 days.

GARLIC PIZZA BREAD

(AMERICAN FAST-FOOD STYLE)

Serves 1

1 tablespoon butter
1 tablespoon olive oil
1 teaspoon garlic powder
Pinch of mixed herbs
Pinch of salt and black pepper
1 prepared 25 cm/10 inch pizza base
2 tablespoons sweet pizza sauce (opposite)
100 g/3½ oz mozzarella cheese, grated
1 small pinch dried oregano

In a small bowl, combine the butter, olive oil, garlic powder, mixed herbs, salt and pepper. Mix well and set aside.

Preheat the pizza stone in the oven for 1 hour at the highest possible heat.

Lightly oil a pizza tray or screen and place the pizza base on top. Spread the pizza sauce onto the pizza base, followed by the prepared garlic butter mixture. Add the mozzarella cheese.

When the pizza stone is preheated, turn the oven down to 200°C/400°F/Gas Mark 6. Place the pizza tray on top of the stone and bake for 8–10 minutes or until the crust becomes golden and the cheese is melted.

Slide the pizza off the tray and directly onto the pizza stone for 3–4 minutes to ensure the base is properly browned if desired.

Remove the pizza from the oven. Garnish with a pinch of dried oregano, slice and serve.

MEAT FEAST PIZZA

(AMERICAN FAST-FOOD STYLE)

Serves 1

1 prepared 25 cm/10 inch pizza base
2–3 tablespoons sweet pizza sauce (page 88)
100 g/3½ oz mozzarella cheese, grated
5–6 slices of pepperoni
1 small handful cooked roast chicken, shredded
2 slices cooked lean bacon, chopped
Pinch of freshly ground black pepper
1 small pinch dried oregano

Preheat the pizza stone in the oven for 1 hour at the highest possible heat.

Lightly oil a pizza tray or screen and place the pizza base on top. Spread the pizza sauce onto the pizza base.

Add the grated mozzarella cheese, pepperoni, roast chicken and bacon.

When the pizza stone is preheated, turn the oven down to 200°C/400°F/Gas Mark 6. Place the pizza tray on top of the stone and bake for 10–12 minutes or until the crust becomes golden and the cheese is melted.

Slide the pizza off the tray and directly onto the pizza stone for 3–4 minutes to ensure the base is properly browned if desired.

Remove the pizza from the oven. Garnish with black pepper and dried oregano, slice and serve.

SPICY CHICKEN AND SWEETCORN PIZZA

(Kebab Shop Style)

Serves 1

1 medium chicken breast fillet (around 85 g/3 oz)
1 teaspoon Cajun spice mix (page 186)
1 tablespoon olive oil
1 teaspoon lemon juice
1 prepared 25 cm/10 inch pizza base
2 tablespoons sweet pizza sauce (page 88)
100 g/3½ oz mozzarella cheese, grated
½ green pepper, finely chopped
Pinch of freshly ground black pepper
1 small pinch dried oregano

Trim any excess fat from the chicken breast. Cut the chicken into bite sized pieces and place in a bowl with the Cajun spice mix, olive oil and lemon juice. Mix well.

Arrange the chicken on a baking tray. Preheat the oven to 150°C/300°F/Gas Mark 2. Bake the chicken for 18–20 minutes or until cooked through. Remove from the oven and set aside to cool. Once cooled, shred the chicken with a knife and fork. The cooked chicken will store well in the fridge for up to 48 hours.

Preheat the pizza stone in the oven for 1 hour at the highest possible heat.

Lightly oil a pizza tray or screen and place the pizza base on top. Spread the pizza sauce onto the pizza base. Add the grated mozzarella cheese, shredded cooked chicken and green pepper. When the pizza stone is preheated, turn the oven down to 200°C/400°F/Gas Mark 6. Place the pizza tray on top of the stone and bake for 10–12 minutes or until the crust becomes golden and the cheese is melted.

Slide the pizza off the tray and directly onto the pizza stone for 3–4 minutes to ensure the base is properly browned if desired.

Remove the pizza from the oven. Garnish with black pepper and dried oregano, slice and serve.

VEGETARIAN VOLCANO PIZZA

(AMERICAN FAST-FOOD STYLE)

Serves 1

2 tablespoons tinned sweetcorn, drained
2 small button mushrooms, finely sliced
¼ green pepper, finely chopped
½ small red onion, finely chopped
1 green finger chilli pepper, finely sliced (see page 62)
1 medium tomato, deseeded and finely chopped
Pinch of cayenne pepper (optional)
1 prepared 25 cm/10 inch pizza base
2 tablespoons sweet pizza sauce (page 88)
100 g/3½ oz mozzarella cheese, grated
Small pinch of freshly ground black pepper
1 small pinch dried oregano

In a small bowl, combine the sweetcorn, mushrooms, green pepper, red onion, finger chilli pepper and tomato. Add the cayenne pepper if desired. Mix well and set aside.

Preheat the pizza stone in the oven for 1 hour at the highest possible heat.

Lightly oil a pizza tray or screen and place the pizza base on top. Spread the pizza sauce onto the pizza base.

Add the grated mozzarella cheese and prepared vegetables.

When the pizza stone is preheated, turn the oven down to 200°C/400°F/Gas Mark 6. Place the pizza tray on top of the stone and bake for 10–12 minutes or until the crust becomes golden and the cheese is melted.

Slide the pizza off the tray and directly onto the pizza stone for 3–4 minutes to ensure the base is properly browned if desired.

Remove the pizza from the oven. Garnish with black pepper and dried oregano, slice and serve.

PEPPERONI, HAM AND MUSHROOM CALZONE

(KEBAB SHOP STYLE)

Serves 1

½ teaspoon olive oil
2 slices lean ham, chopped
3 small button mushrooms, sliced
¼ small onion, finely chopped
1 garlic clove, crushed
Small pinch of freshly ground black pepper
1 prepared 25 cm/10 inch pizza base
4 tablespoons sweet pizza sauce (page 88)
100 g/3½ oz grated mozzarella cheese, plus a little extra for
    topping if desired
5–6 slices of pepperoni

Preheat the pizza stone in the oven for 1 hour at the highest possible heat.

Heat the olive oil in a wok or frying pan over a medium-high heat. Add the chopped ham and sliced mushrooms. Stir-fry for 3–4 minutes.

Add the chopped onion, crushed garlic and black pepper. Stir-fry for a further minute. Pour the cooked ham and mushroom mixture into a bowl and set aside to cool.

Lightly oil a pizza tray or screen and place the pizza base on top. Spread the pizza sauce onto the pizza base. Add the mozzarella cheese and pepperoni slices over one half of the pizza base. Add the prepared ham and mushrooms. Fold the dough over the filling and press down at the edges to form a seal.

When the pizza stone is preheated, turn the oven down to 200°C/400°F/Gas Mark 6. Place the pizza tray onto the pizza stone and bake for around 12–13 minutes or until the calzone is turning golden brown.

Flip the calzone if desired and add a little extra mozzarella cheese over the top if desired. Bake for a further 1–2 minutes or until the cheese melts.

Remove the calzone from the oven and allow to stand for 3–4 minutes before serving.

PIZZA TOAST

(KEBAB SHOP STYLE)

Serves 1

This dish is ideal when time is short and, although simple in its creation, very closely imitates the flavour of a kebab shop pizza, particularly when served with spicy house special chilli sauce (page 149).

2 slices thin white bread
2 large handfuls of grated mozzarella cheese
1 tomato, deseeded and sliced
Pinch of fresh black pepper
Pinch of dried oregano

Grill the bread on one side until golden.

Flip the bread and divide one handful of grated mozzarella cheese over each slice.

Add the tomato slices and cover with the remaining mozzarella cheese. Place the pizza toast back under the grill until the cheese melts and becomes golden.

Switch off the grill and garnish the pizza toast with black pepper and dried oregano. Place the toast back under the grill in order to allow the residual heat to warm the herbs.

Cut the pizza toast into triangles and serve with the above-mentioned chilli sauce, spiced onions or jalapeno peppers.

7

OTHER POPULAR DISHES

The range of dishes available from fast-food and takeaway restaurants is ever growing, offering a variety of foods from around the world. As competition increases, restaurants are required to offer a wider and more diverse selection of meals and so the choice continues to grow.

This chapter includes some of those dishes, from Mexican chilli to Thai green curry, as well as more traditional chip shop favourites such as Special Fish and King Rib.

CHILLI CON CARNE
(Mexican Style)

Serves 6–8

Adding chocolate to a savoury dish may seem strange at first but it's guaranteed to give a smooth, sweet finish to the chilli. A teaspoon or two of sugar will also work well should chocolate not be available. Fresh chilli peppers may be added to the recipe if a hotter chilli is desired. The saying goes, 'If you know beans about chilli, you know chilli ain't got no beans!' While this is undoubtedly true in the traditional sense, most modern takeaway and restaurant chillies do include kidney beans.

1 tablespoon vegetable oil
2 large onions, finely chopped
2 red peppers, finely chopped
4 garlic cloves, crushed
1½ teaspoons cumin powder
1 teaspoon coriander powder
2 teaspoons chilli powder
2 teaspoons paprika
1 kg/2.2 lb beef mince
2 tablespoons tomato purée
1 tablespoon Worcester sauce
2 x 400 g/14 oz tins chopped tomatoes
700 ml/25 fl oz beef stock (or 700 ml/25 fl oz boiling water
    mixed with 1½ beef stock cubes)
1 teaspoon dried oregano
1 cinnamon stick
¼ teaspoon black pepper
2 x 400 g/14 oz tins kidney beans, rinsed and drained
2 squares (around 20 g/1 oz) of good quality dark chocolate
    (minimum 60% cocoa solids)

Heat a large stockpot with the oil over a low-medium heat. Add the chopped onions and stir-fry for 2–3 minutes.

Add the chopped peppers and crushed garlic. Stir-fry for a further 2 minutes.

Add the cumin powder, coriander powder, chilli powder and paprika. Stir-fry for 1 minute and set aside.

Heat a large frying pan over a high heat. Brown the beef mince for 2–3 minutes. Drain any excess oil from the pan and add the tomato purée and Worcester sauce. Stir-fry over a low heat for 3–4 minutes.

Add the beef mince to the stockpot with the vegetables. Add the tinned tomatoes, beef stock, dried oregano, cinnamon stick and black pepper. Mix well and bring to the boil.

When the mixture reaches boiling point, place a tight fitting lid on top, reduce the heat to the lowest available setting and simmer for 10 minutes.

Remove the cinnamon stick and continue to simmer for a further 35 minutes.

Add the kidney beans and chocolate. Mix well. Simmer for a further 15–20 minutes, adding a little water if necessary.

Serve with boiled rice, fried potatoes and sour cream, or as a baked potato topping. Divide any leftover chilli into portion sizes and freeze for future use. The chilli will freeze well for up to 3 months.

CHILLI NON CARNE
(VEGETABLE CHILLI)
(MEXICAN STYLE)

Serves 3–4

2 tablespoons olive oil
½ red pepper, finely chopped
½ green pepper, finely chopped
½ yellow pepper, finely chopped
5 green finger chilli peppers, finely chopped (see page 62)
2 small onions, finely chopped
1 apple, peeled, cored and finely chopped
4 garlic cloves, crushed
1 x 400 g/14 oz tin peeled plum tomatoes
1.2 litres/2 pints water
1 tablespoon chilli powder
1 tablespoon dried Italian herbs
1 teaspoon mixed herbs
1 teaspoon cayenne pepper
½ teaspoon turmeric
Pinch of salt and pinch of black pepper
1 x 400 g/14 oz tin kidney beans, rinsed and drained
Grated Cheddar cheese and raw onion slices

Heat the oil in a large stock pot over a medium heat. Add the red pepper, green pepper, yellow pepper, chilli peppers, onions and apple. Stir-fry for 5–6 minutes.

Add the garlic. Fry for 1 minute.

Add the tinned tomatoes and water. Add the chilli powder, Italian herbs, mixed herbs, cayenne pepper, turmeric, salt and black pepper. Bring to the boil, reduce the heat to low and place a lid on the pan. Simmer for 1½ hours or until the liquid is reduced and the sauce has thickened.

Mash the vegetables until the mixture has a mince like consistency. Add the drained kidney beans and simmer on a low heat for a further 10 minutes.

Serve the vegetable chilli topped with grated Cheddar cheese and raw onion slices. Leftover chilli will store well in the freezer for up to 3 months.

CHICKEN KATSU CURRY

(JAPANESE RESTAURANT STYLE)

Serves 1

If time is short, good Chinese curry sauce mixes such as Yeung's or Maykway provide a quick alternative to the Japanese curry sauce used in this recipe and will deliver good results.

1 large skinless, boneless chicken breast fillet (around 113 g/ 4 oz weight)
Pinch of salt and pinch of black pepper
4 tablespoons plain flour
6 tablespoons panko breadcrumbs (page 181)
1 egg
6 tablespoons vegetable oil

Trim any excess fat from the chicken breast. Wrap the chicken between a folded layer of cling film and use a meat mallet to pound the chicken breast fillet until flat and thin. Season the chicken with the salt and pepper.

Arrange the plain flour and panko breadcrumbs on two separate plates. Whisk the egg in a bowl.

Keeping one hand dry, dip the chicken piece first into the flour, then into the egg and finally into the panko breadcrumbs. Press the breadcrumbs down firmly so that the chicken piece is completely coated. Set aside on a plate.

Heat the oil over a medium heat. Fry the breaded chicken for around 4 minutes. Flip the chicken piece over in the pan and fry on the other side for a further 3–4 minutes or until the breadcrumbs are golden and the chicken is cooked through.

Remove the breaded chicken from the pan and drain off any excess oil. Cut the chicken into 4–6 slices.

Arrange the sliced breaded chicken on the plate. Serve with the Japanese curry sauce (overleaf) and Japanese sticky rice (page 128).

JAPANESE CURRY SAUCE

(JAPANESE RESTAURANT STYLE)

Serves 1

2 teaspoons margarine
½ small onion, finely sliced
1 heaped teaspoon garlic and ginger paste (page 182)
2 teaspoons margarine
1 tablespoon plain flour
1 tablespoon hot Madras curry powder
250 ml/9 fl oz chicken stock
Pinch of garam masala

Heat a non-stick pot over a low heat. Add 2 teaspoons of margarine and the finely sliced onion. Stir-fry for 3–4 minutes or until the onions turn golden brown. Add the garlic and ginger paste and stir-fry for a further minute.

Remove the mixture from the pan and set aside.

Add another 2 teaspoons of margarine to the pot. Add the plain flour and mix well until the mixture forms a paste and the flour is cooked out. Add the curry powder and mix well again. The pan will become very dry at this stage.

Slowly add a third of the chicken stock. Stir constantly and press down with a spatula in order to prevent any lumps from forming in the sauce. Add another third of the chicken stock and mix well. Add the prepared onion/garlic and ginger mixture.

Add the remaining chicken stock and simmer on a low heat for 6–8 minutes or until the sauce is well reduced and thickened. Add the garam masala and simmer for a final 30 seconds.

Serve the curry sauce over chicken katsu curry (page 99) or with rice or chips.

YAKITORI CHICKEN

(JAPANESE RESTAURANT STYLE)

Serves 1–2

6 tablespoons soy sauce (recommended brand: Kikkoman)
1 tablespoon sake
1 teaspoon mirin
1 tablespoon white sugar
2 large skinless, boneless chicken breast fillets (around 113 g/
** 4 oz weight per breast)**
1 teaspoon vegetable oil
1 teaspoon cornflour
6 wooden skewers, soaked for 30 minutes before use
1 leek or 1 large spring onion, cut into small bite sized pieces

In a small pot, combine the soy sauce, sake, mirin and white sugar. Bring to the boil, reduce the heat and stir over a low heat for 3–4 minutes or until the sauce begins to foam and reduces. Set aside to cool.

Trim any excess fat from the chicken breast and cut each breast into 5–6 thin strips. Add 2 teaspoons of the prepared sauce and the vegetable oil. Mix well by hand and marinade for 5 minutes. Add the cornflour and mix well once again. Set aside.

Ribbon the chicken strips onto 4 of the soaked wooden skewers, piercing each piece of chicken several times. Each skewer should comfortably hold 2–3 strips of chicken. Add the leek or spring onion pieces to the remaining 2 skewers.

Heat a griddle pan to a medium-high heat. Brush the chicken and vegetable skewers with a little vegetable oil and place carefully onto the griddle pan. Reduce the heat to medium. Cook the chicken and vegetable skewers on a high heat for 2–3 minutes per side or until the chicken is cooked through and just beginning to char. Baste the skewers frequently with a further 1–2 tablespoons of the remaining sauce during cooking. The skewers will also cook very well on a double-plated health grill.

Remove the cooked chicken skewers and serve as a starter, or with sticky rice as a main meal.

THAI GREEN CURRY

(THAI TAKEAWAY STYLE)

Serves 1–2

1 large skinless, boneless chicken breast fillet (average weight
   113 g/4 oz)
1 red onion
1 tablespoon garlic and ginger paste (page 182)
2 finger chilli peppers (see page 62)
1 stalk of lemongrass
½ teaspoon coriander powder
½ teaspoon cumin powder
½ teaspoon white pepper
1 teaspoon brown sugar
Pinch of salt
1 small handful of fresh basil leaves
1 large handful of fresh coriander leaves and stems
2 tablespoons lime juice
2 teaspoons fish sauce
4 tablespoons coconut milk
2 tablespoons vegetable oil
200 ml/7 fl oz chicken stock (or 200 ml/7 fl oz boiling water
   mixed with ½ chicken stock cube)
2 kaffir lime leaves
200 ml/7 fl oz coconut milk

Trim any excess fat from the chicken breast fillet and cut into bite sized
pieces. Set aside.

In a blender, combine the red onion, garlic and ginger paste, chilli
peppers, lemongrass, coriander powder, cumin powder, white pepper,
brown sugar, salt, fresh basil, fresh coriander, lime juice, fish sauce and 4
tablespoons of coconut milk. Blitz well until fully combined. Set aside.

Heat a wok or frying pan to a medium heat. Add the vegetable oil. Add
the prepared curry paste and stir-fry for 1 minute.

Add the chicken pieces and turn in the pan until fully sealed. Add the chicken stock and bring to the boil. Add the kaffir lime leaves.

Increase the heat to medium-high and cook the sauce for 8–10 minutes, gradually adding the coconut milk until the sauce is slightly thickened and the chicken is just cooked through.

Allow the curry to cool slightly. Serve with fragrant Thai rice.

SPECIAL FISH
(CHIP SHOP STYLE)

Serves 1

1 large haddock or cod fillet
1 egg
4 tablespoons breadcrumbs (recommended brand: Ruskoline)
2 tablespoons vegetable oil
2 lemon slices

Check the fish fillet for any small bones and remove them. Pat the fish dry with kitchen paper.

Whisk the egg in a large bowl and set aside. Spread the breadcrumbs out over a large plate.

Keeping one hand dry, dip the fish fillet into the egg, then into the breadcrumbs. Press down gently so that the crumbs stick to the fish.

Heat the oil in a frying pan over a medium heat. Fry the breaded fish for 2–3 minutes per side or until cooked through and golden.

Remove the fish from the pan, drain off any excess oil and garnish with lemon slices. Season to taste with salt and serve with chips and mushy peas.

KING RIB

(Chip Shop Style)

Serves 1

Roughly 113 g/4 oz pork mince
Large pinch of salt
Large pinch of black pepper
Pinch of sugar
2 tablespoons barbecue sauce (recommended brand: Heinz)
120 g/4 oz plain flour
60 g/2 oz cornflour
Pinch of bicarbonate of soda
1 teaspoon salt
around 200 ml/7 fl oz beer
Oil for deep frying

In a large bowl, combine the mince, salt, black pepper and sugar. Mix well and roll the mince into a ball. Using a sheet of greaseproof paper, flatten the mince into a thin, oval shaped patty. Cover and freeze for at least 2 hours.

Heat a little oil in a pan over a low-medium heat. Place the frozen pork patty into the pan and fry for 5–6 minutes or until just cooked through, turning occasionally. After 4 minutes, baste the pork patty with barbecue sauce on both sides, continuing to turn so that the sauce cooks into the patty.

Remove the pork from the pan and set aside to cool. Once cooled, place in the fridge for at least 1 hour to help the remaining sauce set onto the patty. If desired, the king rib may be prepared to this stage up to 24 hours in advance and finished the next day.

In a large bowl, combine the plain flour, cornflour, bicarbonate of soda and salt. Mix well. Add the beer and whisk thoroughly until a smooth batter is formed. The batter should have the consistency of single cream.

Heat the oil for deep-frying over a medium heat. Drop a half-teaspoon of batter mixture into the oil to test the heat. When fully heated, dip the pork quickly into the batter and drop carefully into the hot oil. Fry for 2–3 minutes or until golden, turning once or twice. Remove the king rib from the pan, drain off any excess oil and season liberally with salt. Serve with chips.

PIRI PIRI CHICKEN

(MEXICAN RESTAURANT STYLE)

Serves 1

This spicy chicken is excellent with Mexican rice or even served inside
a burger bun with lettuce and mayonnaise.

4 tablespoons vegetable oil
½ red pepper, diced
2 garlic cloves, crushed
1 tablespoon white wine vinegar
1–2 finger chilli peppers (see page 62)
½ teaspoon salt
1 teaspoon dried oregano
2 tablespoons lemon juice
2 tablespoons water
**1 large skinless, boneless chicken breast fillet (average weight
    113 g/4 oz)**

Heat the oil in a pan and add the red pepper. Fry over a low heat for
3–4 minutes or until the pepper begins to soften. Add the crushed garlic
and fry for 1 minute.

Add the white wine vinegar, chilli peppers, salt and dried oregano.
Switch off the heat and stir the mixture for 10 seconds. Add the lemon
juice and water and allow the mixture to cool slightly. Pour the mix into
a blender and blitz for 30 seconds or until smooth.

Allow the marinade to cool completely before adding the chicken.

Trim any excess fat from the chicken. Using a meat mallet, pound the
chicken breast between two sheets of cling film until thin.

Add the chicken to the marinade and mix well. Cover and place in the
fridge for at least 1 hour or up to 4 hours if possible.

Heat a griddle pan over a high heat. When the pan is smoking, reduce
the heat to medium-low. Cook the chicken breast for around 2–3
minutes on each side or until charred and cooked through.

Serve with Mexican spicy rice (page 127).

BBQ PULLED PORK

(MEXICAN RESTAURANT STYLE)

Serves 4–6

Smothered in a barbecue sauce made with its own juices, this juicy pork is perfect inside a burger bun or a wrap. Although marinating and baking requires some time, the preparation is easy and once in the oven the pork can be left unattended while cooking.

1 teaspoon dried coriander leaves
2 teaspoons garlic powder
½ teaspoon ginger powder
1 tablespoon paprika
1 tablespoon smoked paprika
1 teaspoon chilli powder
½ teaspoon ground cinnamon
3 tablespoons Demerara sugar
2 teaspoons salt
½ teaspoon black pepper
½ teaspoon white pepper
1.3 kg/3 lb skinless, boneless pork shoulder
500 ml/18 fl oz apple cider
1 tablespoon Demerara sugar
2 teaspoons lemon juice
1 tablespoon honey
1 tablespoon barbecue sauce

In a bowl, combine the dried coriander leaves, garlic powder, ginger powder, paprika, smoked paprika, chilli powder, ground cinnamon, Demerara sugar, salt, black pepper and white pepper. Mix thoroughly and set aside.

Wash the pork shoulder and pat it dry with kitchen paper. Using a fork, stab the meat randomly all over. Rub the prepared spice mixture into the pork until completely coated. Place the marinated meat in a large bowl, cover with cling film and place in the fridge for at least 2 hours or overnight if possible.

Preheat the oven to 150°C/300°F/Gas Mark 2.

Arrange a wire rack over a roasting tray. Pour the apple cider into the roasting tray and arrange the pork on the wire rack above. Cover the roasting tin and wire rack with foil. Place into the oven on the middle shelf and bake for 4–5 hours.

Remove the pork from the oven and pour the juices and apple cider from the roasting tray into a large pot. Scrape the tray well with a spatula to ensure all of the meat juices are collected.

Clean out the roasting tray (or use a second tray) and once again place the meat over the tray on a wire rack.

Increase the oven temperature to 200°C/400°F/Gas Mark 6. Return the pork to the oven and cook for a further 30–40 minutes.

Meanwhile, heat the pot with the collected juices on a low heat for 2–3 minutes. Add 1 tablespoon of Demerara sugar and 2 teaspoons of lemon juice. Mix well, add the honey and barbecue sauce and simmer until thick.

When the meat is cooked, remove it from the oven and set aside to cool for 5 minutes. Using two forks (or by hand), shred the pork.

Add the shredded pork to the pot and continue simmering until the mixture becomes thick and syrupy.

Serve the pulled pork in toasted burger buns, or in a wrap with Mexican spicy rice (page 127). Leftover pulled pork will freeze well for up to 1 month.

8

SIDES, SALADS, SOUPS, SNACKS AND SAUCES

It's often difficult to choose your favourite takeaway dish, especially with so much choice on the menu. Many dishes complement each other and so, for example, when creating a Chinese dish it's essential to accompany it with egg fried rice or noodles. Kebabs need chilli sauce, pizza crusts need garlic, and herb dips, while Indian curry dishes are just begging to be mopped up with delicious chapati and paratha breads.

The recipes included in this chapter are perfect as an introduction or accompaniment to your main meal dishes and can often be prepared in advance, ensuring that you're able to offer a wide range of dishes to your guests.

Also included are snacks designed to recreate foods often sold in cinemas at hugely inflated prices. Using these recipes, classic movie accompaniments such as popcorn can be prepared for no more than a few pence per portion, perhaps leaving money which can be spent on further recreating the experience by adding to your home cinema set-up!

MUSHROOM PAKORA
(Kebab Shop Style)

Serves 1–2

Small button mushrooms are perfect for use in this dish. The garlic and smoked paprika seasoning in the pakora batter combines perfectly with the mushrooms.

5 tablespoons gram flour
½ teaspoon garlic powder
½ teaspoon smoked paprika
½ teaspoon salt
¼ teaspoon garam masala
¼ teaspoon coriander powder
½ teaspoon cumin powder
Pinch of turmeric
Pinch of chilli powder
½ teaspoon dried fenugreek leaves
1 small handful fresh coriander leaves and stalks, finely chopped
60–75 ml/2–2¼ fl oz water
Oil for deep frying
10–12 small button mushrooms

In a large bowl, combine the gram flour, garlic powder, smoked paprika, salt, garam masala, coriander powder, cumin powder, turmeric, chilli powder, dried fenugreek leaves and fresh coriander. Mix well. Add the water a little at a time until a smooth, slightly thick batter is created. The consistency should be similar to that of double cream.

Heat the oil on a medium-high heat. Dip each button mushroom into the pakora batter and place carefully into the pan. Fry for 2 minutes.

Remove the mushroom pakora pieces from the pan and set aside on a plate for 2 minutes. This will allow the mushrooms to cook through without overbrowning the batter. Return the mushroom pakora to the pan and fry for a further 1–2 minutes or until crispy and golden.

Remove the mushroom pakora from the pan and drain off any excess oil. Serve with onion salad (page 125) and minted yogurt dip (page 147).

HAGGIS PAKORA

(KEBAB SHOP STYLE)

Serves 1–2

Scotland's influence on Indian takeaway food continues to grow, with haggis pakora now a firm favourite on most Indian menus.

5 tablespoons gram flour
½ teaspoon salt
¼ teaspoon garam masala
¼ teaspoon coriander powder
¼ teaspoon cumin powder
Pinch of turmeric
Pinch of chilli powder
½ teaspoon dried fenugreek leaves
60–75 ml/2–2½ fl oz water
3 pieces sliced haggis (recommended brand: Halls)
Oil for deep frying

In a large bowl, combine the gram flour, salt, garam masala, coriander powder, cumin powder, turmeric, chilli powder and dried fenugreek leaves. Mix well.

Add the water a little at a time until a smooth, slightly thick batter is created. The consistency should be similar to that of double cream.

Cut each haggis slice into 4 pieces.

Heat the oil on a medium-high heat. Dip each piece of haggis into the pakora batter and place carefully into the pan. Fry for around 3–4 minutes or until the batter is crisp and golden.

Remove the haggis pakora from the pan and drain off any excess oil. Serve with onion salad (page 125) and house special chilli sauce (page 149).

ONION BHAJI RINGS

(KEBAB SHOP STYLE)

Serves 1–2

1 large Spanish onion
5 tablespoons gram flour
1 teaspoon salt
¼ teaspoon cumin seeds
½ teaspoon coriander powder
Pinch of garam masala
Pinch of chilli powder
1 tablespoon fresh coriander, finely chopped
60–75 ml/2–2½ fl oz water
Oil for deep frying

Peel the Spanish onion and slice into rings. Separate the rings, reserving all of the large and medium sized outer rings. The smaller inner rings may be used also but will fry much more quickly than the outer rings. Restaurants typically use the outer rings and keep the smaller inner rings for use in other dishes where onion is required.

Place the large and medium onion rings in a bowl of cold water. Set aside for 30 minutes.

In a large bowl, combine the gram flour, salt, cumin seeds, coriander powder, garam masala, chilli powder and fresh coriander. Mix thoroughly.

Add the water a little at a time until a smooth, slightly thick batter is created. The consistency should be similar to that of double cream.

Heat the oil on a medium-high heat. Drain the onion rings and pat dry with kitchen paper. Dip each onion ring into the pakora batter and place carefully into the pan. Fry over a high heat for 2–3 minutes or until the batter turns golden and crisp.

Remove the onion bhaji rings from the pan, drain off any excess oil and serve with lemon slices.

GARLIC MUSHROOMS
IN CREAM SAUCE
(KEBAB SHOP STYLE)

Serves 1

Fried mushrooms smothered in a garlic, cheese and cream sauce. Supermarkets sell an inexpensive 'dried Italian cheese' that is acceptable for use in this dish and is far less costly than Parmesan cheese.

75 ml/2½ fl oz double cream
75ml/2½ fl oz semi-skimmed milk
¾ teaspoon cornflour
2 teaspoons vegetable oil
10–12 small button mushrooms, sliced
¼ small onion, finely chopped
2 garlic cloves, crushed
1 tablespoon grated Parmesan cheese or dried Italian cheese
Pinch of black pepper

In a bowl, combine the double cream, semi-skimmed milk and cornflour. Mix well.

Heat the oil in a large wok or frying pan over a medium heat. Add the button mushrooms and stir-fry for 2–3 minutes.

Add the onion and garlic and stir-fry for 1 minute. Reduce the heat to low.

Mix the cream/milk mixture thoroughly again and add it to the pan. Add the cheese and black pepper and mix well.

Cook for 2–3 minutes or until the sauce thickens. Pour the garlic mushrooms into a foil tray and serve.

SPICY POTATO WEDGES
(Kebab Shop Style)

Serves 1

2 large potatoes (recommended variety: Maris Peer)
1 tablespoon vegetable oil
½ teaspoon chilli powder
½ teaspoon cumin powder
1 teaspoon plain flour
Pinch of salt
Pinch of black pepper

Preheat the oven to 220°C/425°F/Gas Mark 7.

Wash and dry the potatoes, leaving the skin on. Cut each potato in half lengthways, then cut into quarters. Slice each quarter once more to create 8 wedges per potato.

Place the potato wedges in a bowl and add the vegetable oil, chilli powder, cumin powder, plain flour, salt and black pepper. Mix well.

Arrange the potatoes on a baking tray and cook in the middle of the oven for 35–40 minutes or until cooked through, turning occasionally.

Serve with sour cream and chive dip (page 148).

CHILLI POPPERS

(KEBAB SHOP STYLE)

Serves 1–2

8 tablespoons panko breadcrumbs (page 181)
1 teaspoon garlic powder
¼ teaspoon onion powder
¼ teaspoon salt
¼ teaspoon paprika
1 teaspoon dried Italian herbs
4 jalapeno peppers or any large, mild chilli peppers (see page 62)
2 tablespoons soft cheese
2 tablespoons grated mozzarella cheese
8 tablespoons plain flour
1 egg, mixed with 4 tablespoons semi–skimmed milk
Oil for deep frying

In a large bowl, combine the panko breadcrumbs, garlic powder, onion powder, salt, paprika and dried Italian herbs. Mix thoroughly and set aside.

Chop the chilli peppers in half. Squeeze and roll the chilli peppers between your fingers over a plate in order to remove the seeds. If a softer texture is desired, pour boiling water over the chilli peppers and drain before continuing as below.

Combine the soft cheese and grated mozzarella in a bowl. Mix well and use a teaspoon to fill the chilli peppers with the cheese mixture.

Keeping one hand dry, dip the filled chilli peppers first into the plain flour, then into the egg and milk mixture and finally into the seasoned breadcrumbs. Set aside for 5 minutes and repeat the process again to ensure all of the chilli peppers are fully coated in the breadcrumb mixture.

Deep-fry the breaded chilli poppers in hot oil on a medium-high heat for 3–4 minutes or until the breadcrumbs are golden brown and crisp. Remove the chilli poppers from the pan, drain off any excess oil and serve.

PARATHA BREAD

(INDIAN RESTAURANT STYLE)

Makes 4 paratha breads

Every Indian curry deserves to be mopped up with some delicious bread. This crisp, flaky bread fits the bill perfectly.

250 g/8 oz chapati flour
Pinch of baking powder
Large pinch of salt
2 tablespoons natural yogurt
Around 120 ml/4 fl oz water
3–4 tablespoons melted butter or ghee

In a bowl, combine the chapati flour, baking powder and salt. Mix well. Add the yogurt and mix well once again. Add the water a little at a time and mix until the dough comes together.

Empty the dough onto a floured surface. Knead the dough for 2–3 minutes or until smooth. Return the dough to the bowl, cover with a damp cloth and set aside to rest for 30 minutes.

Divide the dough into four equal pieces. Roll each piece of dough into a ball. On a floured surface, carefully roll the dough ball out into a 15–20 cm/6–8 inch circle.

Brush the rolled out paratha bread with melted butter or ghee. Roll the bread up like a sausage and, using floured hands, form into a dough ball once again. Roll the dough out again into a 20 cm/8 inch circle. This creates a layer of fat within the dough similar to that made when preparing pastry.

Heat a tava pan over a medium-high heat until just beginning to smoke. Lower the heat to medium-low and place the rolled out paratha bread onto the pan. Cook the paratha bread for around 1 minute, turning every 10–15 seconds. Lower the heat a little and brush both sides of the paratha bread with melted butter or ghee. Continue to cook for a further 2 minutes, again turning every 10–15 seconds and pressing down with a spatula until cooked. Repeat the cooking process with the remaining breads and serve with any Indian curry dish.

ALOO PARATHA

(Indian Restaurant Style)

Makes 4 aloo paratha breads

1 large potato
Pinch of salt
Pinch of cumin powder
Pinch of chilli powder
Pinch of salt and pinch of black pepper
1 tablespoon fresh coriander, finely chopped
½ teaspoon lemon juice or lemon dressing
4 prepared paratha bread dough pieces (page 115)
Chapati flour for dusting
3–4 tablespoons melted butter or ghee

Fill a large pot with water. Peel the potato and chop into two large pieces. Add to the pan with a pinch of salt and bring to the boil. Boil the potato for 15–20 minutes or until soft.

Drain the water and return the pan to the heat. Reduce the heat to low and add the cumin powder, chilli powder, salt and black pepper. Mash the potato mixture thoroughly. Switch off the heat and add the fresh coriander and lemon juice or lemon dressing. Mix well once again then set aside to cool.

Taking one paratha dough piece, roll out the dough to form a 20 cm/8 inch circle. Take one quarter of the potato mixture and place it in the centre of the dough. Wrap the dough around the filling and twist so that the potato mixture is sealed within the dough. Dust the stuffed paratha bread with a little chapati flour and roll out once again.

Heat a tava pan over a medium-high heat until just beginning to smoke. Lower the heat to medium and place the rolled out paratha bread onto the pan. Cook the paratha bread for around 1 minute, turning every 10–15 seconds. Lower the heat a little and brush both sides of the paratha bread with melted butter or ghee. Continue to cook for a further 2 minutes, again turning every 10–15 seconds and pressing down with a spatula until cooked.

Repeat the cooking process with the remaining breads and serve with any Indian curry dish.

PURI BREAD

(INDIAN RESTAURANT STYLE)

Makes 4 puri breads

This silky fried Indian bread is an important part of the hugely popular chicken/chickpea puri starter dishes and is also an excellent accompaniment to any Indian curry.

75 g/3 oz plain white flour
50 g/2 oz wholemeal bread flour
Pinch of salt
Pinch of baking powder
1 tablespoon semi-skimmed milk
Around 50 ml/2 fl oz water
Oil for deep frying

In a large bowl, combine the plain flour, wholemeal flour, salt and baking powder. Mix well. Add the milk and water and mix well with a fork until the dough comes together. Empty the dough onto a floured surface and knead for 3–4 minutes until smooth. Add a little more flour while kneading if necessary to prevent the dough from sticking.

Form the dough into a ball and place in a bowl. Cover with a damp cloth and set aside for 5 minutes. Divide the dough into 4 pieces. Flatten each dough ball into a circle. Use a rolling pin to roll out each piece of dough into a 15 cm/6 inch round puri.

Heat the oil over a medium heat. When the oil is hot, carefully place the rolled out puri into the pan. Immediately press down gently with a spatula and spoon a little oil over the top of the puri. The bread will puff up within seconds.

Let the bread fry for around 20–30 seconds, then carefully flip the bread over to the other side. Fry for a further 20–30 seconds and remove from the pan. As the puri breads are cooked, drain them on kitchen paper and then wrap in foil until ready for use. The breads can be served straight away or stored for several hours and served at room temperature.

Serve as part of chicken/chickpea puri or with any Indian curry dish.

TAVA CHAPATI BREAD

(INDIAN RESTAURANT STYLE)

Makes 4 large chapati breads

250 g/8 oz chapati flour
Pinch of salt
Pinch of bicarbonate of soda
2 tablespoons natural yogurt
Around 120 ml/4 fl oz water

In a large bowl, combine the chapati flour, salt and bicarbonate of soda. Mix well. Add the natural yogurt and mix well once again.

Slowly add the water and mix well with a fork until the dough comes together. All of the water may not be needed. When the dough comes together, empty onto a floured surface and knead for 3–4 minutes until smooth. Add a little more flour while kneading if necessary to prevent the dough from sticking.

Form the dough into a ball and place in a bowl. Cover with a damp cloth and set aside for 45 minutes.

Divide the dough into 4 large pieces. Flatten each dough ball into a circle. Use a rolling pin to roll out each piece into a 25 cm/10 inch round chapati.

Heat a tava pan over a medium-high heat until smoking. Reduce the heat slightly and place the chapati onto the pan.

Cook the chapati for 20 seconds. Flip the bread and continue to cook for a further 1–2 minutes, flipping the bread every 10–15 seconds until cooked and charred spots develop across the surface of the bread.

Remove the chapati from the tava pan and cover loosely with foil. Repeat the process with the remaining dough until all of the breads are cooked.

CHANA PURI

(INDIAN RESTAURANT STYLE)

Serves 1

This chickpea based dish is quick and simple to prepare as well as being a great source of protein.

2 cooked puri breads (page 117)
2 tablespoons onion salad (page 125)
1 tablespoon vegetable oil
½ small onion, finely chopped
½ teaspoon garlic and ginger paste (page 182)
1 tablespoon tomato purée, mixed with 2 tablespoons water
1 heaped teaspoon mild curry paste (recommended brand: Patak's)
1 teaspoon restaurant spice mix (page 181)
Pinch of chilli powder
Pinch of salt
1 teaspoon dried fenugreek leaves
½ tin (around 200 g/7 oz) peeled plum tomatoes, blended
200 ml/7 fl oz water
1 x 400 g/14 oz tin chickpeas, rinsed and drained
½ tomato, sliced
1 small handful fresh coriander leaves, finely chopped
½ lemon, sliced

In a large serving tray, arrange the cooked puri breads. Arrange the onion salad in one corner of the tray.

Heat the oil in a large wok or frying pan over a medium heat. Add the onion and garlic and ginger paste. Stir-fry for 30 seconds. Add the tomato purée and water mixture, curry paste, restaurant spice mix, chilli powder, salt and dried fenugreek leaves. Stir-fry for 30 seconds then add the tinned tomatoes and water. Increase the heat to medium-high and cook for 3–4 minutes. Add the drained chickpeas and mix well.

Add the sliced tomato and half of the coriander leaves. Mix well and continue to cook for a further 2–3 minutes or until the sauce thickens. Pour the chickpeas and sauce over the puri breads and garnish with the remaining coriander. Serve with lemon slices.

VEGETABLE SAMOSAS

(INDIAN RESTAURANT STYLE)

Serves 2–3

1 teaspoon salt
¼ teaspoon cumin powder
¼ teaspoon cumin seeds
¼ teaspoon coriander powder
½ teaspoon garam masala
¼ teaspoon chilli powder
Pinch of turmeric
2 potatoes
2 tablespoons vegetable oil
5 tablespoons frozen peas
1 green finger chilli pepper, finely chopped (see page 62)
½ teaspoon lemon juice or lemon dressing
3 sheets of filo pastry, spring roll wrappers or samosa wrappers
1 tablespoon cornflour mixed with 2 tablespoons water
Vegetable oil for deep frying

In a small bowl, combine the salt, cumin powder, cumin seeds, coriander powder, garam masala, chilli powder and turmeric. Mix well and set aside.

Peel the potatoes and place them in a large pot of water. Add a small pinch of salt and bring the pot to the boil over a high heat. Boil the potatoes for 7–8 minutes or until just slightly soft. Remove from the heat, drain the potatoes and set aside until completely cool.

When the potatoes have cooled, chop them into small cubes. Heat the 2 tablespoons of vegetable oil in a large wok or frying pan over a medium heat. Add the cubed potatoes and frozen peas. Stir-fry for 3–4 minutes.

Lower the heat slightly and add the chopped chilli pepper and prepared spices. Mix thoroughly and stir-fry for 2 minutes.

Add the lemon juice or lemon dressing and stir-fry for a further 30 seconds. Remove the vegetables from the heat and set aside until completely cool. At this stage, the prepared vegetables may be stored in the fridge for up to 24 hours before use.

To cook the samosas, cut the filo pastry, spring roll wrappers or samosa pastry into 3 pieces to create 9 long strips.

Place a teaspoon of the vegetable samosa filling on the bottom corner of one strip. Folding each corner towards the opposite edge in a triangular shape, work towards the top of the strip, using the cornflour mixture as needed to help seal the samosas. Repeat the process until all of the samosas are prepared.

Heat the vegetable oil to a medium heat. Fry the samosas for around 2–3 minutes, turning occasionally until the samosas become golden and crispy. Serve warm or at room temperature.

LAMB SAMOSAS
(INDIAN RESTAURANT STYLE)

Serves 2–3

This mildly spiced mince mixture can also be used to stuff paratha breads in the same way described for aloo parathas (page 116)

½ teaspoon mild Madras curry powder
½ teaspoon turmeric powder
½ teaspoon cumin seeds
Pinch of chilli powder
¼ teaspoon salt
Pinch of black pepper
250 g/8 oz lamb mince
½ onion, finely chopped
1 garlic clove, crushed
1 finger chilli, deseeded and finely chopped (see page 62)
1 tablespoon freshly chopped coriander leaves
½ teaspoon lemon juice
4 sheets of filo pastry, spring roll wrappers or prepared
    samosa pastry
1 tablespoon cornflour, mixed with 2 tablespoons water
Vegetable oil for deep frying

In a small bowl, combine the curry powder, turmeric powder, cumin seeds, chilli powder, salt and black pepper. Set aside.

Heat a wok or frying pan over a medium-high heat. Add the lamb mince to the pan and stir well to break up the mince. Brown the mince over a high heat for 1–2 minutes.

Drain off any excess fat and return to the pan. Lower the heat to medium and add the onion, garlic and chilli. Stir-fry for 1 minute.

Add the prepared spice mix and stir-fry for a further 2 minutes. Switch off the heat and add the chopped coriander and lemon juice. Mix well once again and set the filling aside to cool.

To cook the samosas, cut the filo pastry, spring roll wrappers or samosa pastry into 3 pieces to create 12 long strips.

Place a teaspoon of the lamb samosa filling on the bottom corner of one strip. Folding each corner towards the opposite edge in a triangular shape, work towards the top of the strip, using the cornflour mixture as needed to help seal the samosas. Repeat the process until all of the samosas are prepared.

Heat the vegetable oil to a medium heat. Fry the samosas for around 2–3 minutes, turning occasionally until the samosas become golden and crispy. Serve hot.

ALOO TIKKI

(INDIAN RESTAURANT STYLE)

Serves 1–2 (Makes 4 aloo tikki)

These spiced potato patties are an excellent starter before any curry dish.

3 medium potatoes
1 green finger chilli pepper, chopped (see page 62)
Pinch of turmeric
Pinch of chilli powder
Pinch of cumin powder
Pinch of garam masala
Pinch of garlic powder
Pinch of ginger powder
¼ teaspoon salt
1 small handful chopped fresh coriander
1 egg
6 tablespoons breadcrumbs (recommended brand: Ruskoline)
Oil for deep frying

Cut each potato into 2 pieces and add to a large pan of salted water. Boil the potatoes for 15 minutes or until soft.

Drain the potatoes and return to the pan. Add the chilli pepper, turmeric, chilli powder, cumin powder, garam masala, garlic powder, ginger powder and salt. Mash the potato mixture thoroughly. Add the chopped fresh coriander and mix well once again. Allow the mixture to cool slightly then form into 4 round patties.

Whisk the egg in a small bowl and arrange the breadcrumbs on a plate. Carefully dip the potato patties first into the egg mixture, then into the breadcrumbs. Place the breaded patties onto a plate, cover and place in the fridge for 2 hours or overnight if desired. This will help the coating stick to the patties when fried.

When ready to cook, heat the oil over a medium heat. Fry the aloo tikki for around 2 minutes on each side or until golden and crisp. Drain off any excess oil and serve the aloo tikki with onion salad (opposite).

ONION SALAD
(INDIAN RESTAURANT STYLE)

Serves 1–2

This classic onion salad is served with almost every dish at kebab shops up and down the country.

2 medium onions
¼ cucumber
1 large tomato
1 teaspoon mint sauce
Pinch of salt

Peel and finely slice the onions. Place in a bowl of cold water for around 30 minutes. Drain well through a sieve and pat the onion dry with kitchen paper. Place the dried onion slices in a large bowl.

Slice the cucumber in half and use a teaspoon to scrape out and discard the seeds. Finely chop the cucumber and combine with the onions.

Quarter the tomato and use a knife to carefully remove the seeds. Finely chop the tomato flesh and combine with the onion and cucumber. Mix thoroughly.

Add the teaspoon of mint sauce. Mix thoroughly once more and set aside in the fridge for at least 1 hour before use. Season with salt just before serving.

Serve with chicken/chickpea puri (pages 70/119) or with any Indian curry, kebab or pakora.

VARIATION: CABBAGE AND ONION SALAD

Shred 4 white or red cabbage leaves and place in a bowl with 50 ml (2 fl oz) white vinegar and ½ teaspoon of salt. Soak for at least 1 hour. Rinse the cabbage with water and pat dry. Coat with 1 teaspoon of olive oil and add to the prepared onion salad.

INDIAN FRIED RICE

(INDIAN RESTAURANT STYLE)

Serves 1–2

This savoury, mildly spiced side dish is perfect with any Indian curry.

1 tablespoon vegetable oil
½ small onion, finely chopped
¼ teaspoon garlic and ginger paste (page 182)
½ teaspoon dried fenugreek leaves
¼ teaspoon salt
1 teaspoon restaurant spice mix (page 181)
1 portion precooked rice (page 188)

Heat a wok or frying pan to a high heat. Add the vegetable oil, chopped onion, garlic and ginger paste, dried fenugreek leaves and salt. Stir-fry for 2–3 minutes.

Add the restaurant spice mix and stir-fry thoroughly for 30 seconds. Add the precooked rice and stir-fry for a further 3–4 minutes or until the rice is fully heated through.

Serve the fried rice with any Indian curry.

VARIATIONS:

Mushroom Rice – Add 5–6 small button mushrooms, sliced, at the frying stage with the onion, etc.

Mixed Vegetable Rice – Add 4 tablespoons frozen mixed vegetables (broccoli, cauliflower, carrots, peas) at the frying stage with the onion, etc.

MEXICAN SPICY RICE

(MEXICAN STYLE)

Serves 1–2

1 small onion, finely chopped
½ red pepper, finely chopped
2 tablespoons tinned kidney beans, rinsed and drained
1 tablespoon sweetcorn
1 garlic clove, crushed
1 tomato, deseeded and finely chopped
2 tablespoons finely chopped jarred jalapeno peppers
½ teaspoon cumin powder
¼ teaspoon turmeric powder
¼ teaspoon salt
Pinch of white sugar
¼ teaspoon dried oregano
Pinch of smoked paprika
1 tablespoon vegetable oil
1 portion precooked rice (page 188)

In a large bowl, combine the onion, red pepper, kidney beans, sweetcorn, garlic, tomato and jalapeno peppers. Set aside.

In a separate bowl, combine the cumin powder, turmeric powder, salt, sugar, oregano and paprika. Set aside.

Heat a wok or frying pan to a high heat. Add the vegetable oil. Add the prepared vegetables and stir-fry for 3–4 minutes.

Add the prepared spice mix and continue to stir-fry for a further minute.

Add the precooked rice. Stir-fry for a further 3–4 minutes or until the rice and vegetables become dry and the rice is fully heated through.

Serve the spicy rice with any Mexican dish.

JAPANESE STICKY RICE

(JAPANESE RESTAURANT STYLE)

Serves 1–2

125 g/4 oz sushi rice
160 ml/5½ fl oz water

Wash the rice in cold water and set aside for 5 minutes.

Drain the rice and replace the water with fresh water once again and leave for a further 10 minutes.

Rinse the rice a final time and allow to drain through a sieve. Add the rice to a pan with a tight fitting lid along with the water. Leave the lid off the pan for now.

On a high heat, bring the rice to boiling point. Place the lid on the pan, reduce the heat to low and simmer for 12 minutes or until the liquid has been absorbed.

Switch off the heat and set aside with the lid on for at least 15–20 minutes or until ready to serve.

EGG FRIED RICE

(Chinese Takeaway Style)

Serves 1–2

1 egg
½ teaspoon toasted sesame oil
2 tablespoons vegetable oil
1 portion of precooked rice (page 188)
2 teaspoons soy sauce (recommended brand: Kikkoman) OR 1
    teaspoon each of both light and dark soy sauce
Pinch of salt
1 spring onion, finely sliced (optional)

In a small bowl, combine the egg and toasted sesame oil. Whisk thoroughly.

Heat 1 tablespoon of vegetable oil in a wok or frying pan over a high heat. Add the egg mixture and allow to set in the pan briefly. Cook for 1 minute, breaking up the egg into small pieces with a spatula. Remove the cooked egg and set aside.

Reduce the heat to medium. Add the remaining tablespoon of vegetable oil to the pan. Add the precooked rice and immediately stir-fry to ensure all of the grains of rice are coated in oil.

Stir-fry over a medium heat for 2–3 minutes. Add the soy sauce and salt and stir-fry for a further minute or until the rice is dry and fully reheated.

Pour the rice into a serving tray and garnish with spring onion if desired. Serve with any Chinese dish.

MEAT SPRING ROLLS

(Chinese Takeaway Style)

Serves 2 (Makes 4–6 meat spring rolls)

These pancake rolls can be prepared and wrapped in advance and will take just a few minutes to fry before serving as part of your Chinese meal.

**1 small skinless, boneless chicken breast fillet (around 85 g/
    3 oz weight)**
1 teaspoon oyster sauce
½ teaspoon cornflour
3 small button mushrooms, finely sliced
1 large handful bean sprouts
1 small onion, sliced
½ small carrot, peeled into thin strips
1 tablespoon vegetable oil
1 teaspoon soy sauce
Pinch of salt and pepper seasoning (page 183)
Pinch of Chinese 5-spice
2 tablespoons water
1 small handful cooked, shredded Chinese char siu (optional)
1 small handful cooked prawns, chopped (optional)
4–6 spring roll wrappers
1 tablespoon cornflour, mixed with 2 tablespoons water
Oil for deep frying

Trim any excess fat from the chicken breast and cut into small, thin strips. Place the chicken strips into a bowl, add the oyster sauce and cornflour and mix well. Set aside for 5 minutes.

In a large bowl, combine the sliced mushrooms, bean sprouts, sliced onion and carrot strips.

Heat the oil in a large wok or frying pan over a high heat. Add the chicken pieces to the wok and stir-fry for 3-4 minutes or until just cooked through. Remove and set aside.

Add a little more oil to the pan and add the prepared vegetables. Stir-fry for 2 minutes. Add the soy sauce, salt and pepper seasoning, Chinese 5-spice and water. Mix thoroughly and stir-fry for a further minute, mixing the ingredients well.

Return the chicken pieces to the pan and mix thoroughly once more. Pour the prepared filling into a large bowl and set aside to cool completely. When the mixture has cooled, add the char siu and cooked prawns if desired and mix well once again.

Take a small handful of the filling mixture and place it close to the bottom of the spring roll wrapper. Fold the bottom of the wrapper over the filling and then fold in both the left and right edges and continue rolling towards the top of the wrapper.

Brush the top of the pancake roll wrapper with a little of the cornflour and water mixture. Seal the spring roll tightly. At this stage the spring rolls may be refrigerated until ready for use.

Deep fry the spring rolls in hot oil over a medium-high heat for 3–4 minutes or until golden. Drain off any excess oil and arrange the cooked pancake rolls on a wire rack over a baking tray for 2–3 minutes. This will ensure that the pastry batter does not become soggy.

Serve the pancake rolls with sweet chilli sauce (page 183) or as a side dish with any Chinese meal.

CHICKEN AND SWEETCORN SOUP

(CHINESE TAKEAWAY STYLE)

Serves 1–2

1 egg
350 ml/12 fl oz Chinese stock (page 185) or chicken stock
1 large handful cooked roast chicken, shredded
3–4 tablespoons tinned creamed sweetcorn
Dash of soy sauce (recommended brand: Kikkoman)
2 teaspoons cornflour mixed with 2 tablespoons water
1 spring onion, finely sliced
Dash of toasted sesame oil

Crack the egg and move the yolk between the shell halves several times, catching the egg white in a small bowl. Discard the yolk. Whisk the egg white thoroughly and set aside.

Heat the stock in a wok or pot until boiling. Reduce to a simmer and add the cooked chicken and tinned creamed sweetcorn. Mix well and simmer for 2 minutes.

Add the dash of soy sauce and mix well again. Add the cornflour and water mixture and mix through the soup to thicken slightly. Simmer for a further 2 minutes.

Slowly drizzle in the whisked egg white, stirring slowly. Simmer for a further 30 seconds.

Pour the soup into a serving bowl and garnish with the spring onion. Add the toasted sesame oil and serve.

DEEP FRIED WONTONS
(Chinese Takeaway Style)

Serves 2

150 g/5 oz raw prawns, peeled and chopped
½ teaspoon dry sherry
1 teaspoon soy sauce
2 teaspoons fish sauce
½ teaspoon oyster sauce
Pinch of ginger powder
Pinch of sugar
Dash of toasted sesame oil
6–8 wonton wrappers
oil for deep frying

In a large bowl, combine the prawns, sherry, soy sauce, fish sauce, oyster sauce, ginger powder, sugar and sesame oil. Mix thoroughly.

Place the mixture in the fridge for 1 hour.

Fill the wonton wrappers with a spoonful of the filling and twist the top to seal the mixture in. Heat the oil for deep-frying and fry the wontons over a medium heat for 3–4 minutes or until crispy and the filling is cooked through.

Drain off any excess oil and serve the wontons with sweet chilli sauce (page 183).

CURRY PUFFS

(CHINESE TAKEAWAY STYLE)

Serves 2–3

Crispy triangles with just a hint of curry flavour, these snack–sized puffs are an ideal starter to any Chinese meal.

1 large potato, peeled and diced
1 small carrot, peeled and diced
2 tablespoons frozen peas
2 teaspoons vegetable oil
¼ teaspoon salt
1 heaped teaspoon mild Madras curry powder
6 frozen spring roll wrappers
1 tablespoon cornflour
2 tablespoons water
Vegetable oil for deep frying

In a large pot, combine the diced potato and carrot. Cover with plenty of water, bring to the boil and simmer for 5–6 minutes.

Add the frozen peas and continue to simmer the vegetables for a further 3 minutes.

Remove the vegetables from the pan and drain well.

Heat a wok or frying pan to a medium heat. Add the 2 teaspoons of vegetable oil and pour the drained vegetables into the pan. Stir-fry for 2–3 minutes.

Add the salt and Madras curry powder. Stir-fry for a further 2 minutes or until the spices have cooked through.

Remove the vegetables from the heat and mash well. Set aside to cool.

Defrost the spring roll wrappers according to the packet's instructions. While working with the wrappers, keep unused wrappers covered with a damp cloth until needed.

Mix the tablespoon of cornflour and 2 tablespoons of water in a small cup. This mixture can be used like a glue to help seal the curry puffs.

Cut each wrapper into three strips. Place a teaspoon of the vegetable mixture on the bottom corner of one strip. Folding each corner towards the opposite edge, work towards the top of the strip, using the cornflour mixture as needed to help seal the curry puffs.

The prepared curry puffs may be fried immediately or covered and set aside in the fridge for up to 24 hours.

Heat the vegetable oil to a medium heat. Fry the curry puffs for around 3–4 minutes, turning occasionally until the curry puffs become golden and crispy.

Serve with sweet chilli sauce (page 183).

SALT AND PEPPER CHIPS
(Chinese Takeaway Style)

Serves 1

This spicy variation on traditional chips has become hugely popular in recent years. To replicate the takeaway dish perfectly, try to source frozen chips from good Chinese supermarkets. Modern day 'air fryer' machines such as Tefal's 'ActiFry' are ideal for preparing takeaway style chips. Less oil is required to cook chips using these machines and the chips can be left to cook themselves for around 20–25 minutes without supervision, leaving ideal time to prepare other dishes and accompaniments.

½ red pepper, finely sliced
½ green pepper, finely sliced
1 small onion, finely sliced
2 garlic cloves, finely sliced
1 finger chilli pepper, finely sliced (see page 62)
1 large portion frozen chips (recommended brand: Farm
    Frites)
1 teaspoon vegetable oil
Around ¼ teaspoon salt and pepper seasoning (page 183)
¼ teaspoon toasted sesame oil

In a large bowl, combine the red pepper, green pepper and onion. Set aside.

In a separate bowl, combine the garlic and chilli. Set aside.

Cook the chips according to instructions. When the chips are almost cooked, heat the vegetable oil in a large wok or frying pan over a medium–high heat. Add the red pepper, green pepper and onion. Stir-fry for 2–3 minutes or until the vegetables just begin to soften.

Add the garlic and chilli to the pan. Stir-fry for a further 30 seconds. The pan should begin to become dry once again.

Add the cooked chips and season well to taste with the salt and pepper seasoning. Stir-fry for a further 1–2 minutes.

Switch off the heat and add the toasted sesame oil. Mix well once more and serve as a side dish with any Chinese meal.

PLAIN CHOW MEIN NOODLES
(CHINESE TAKEAWAY STYLE)

Serves 1

1 nest egg noodles
1 teaspoon vegetable oil
2 teaspoons soy sauce (recommended brand: Kikkoman) OR 1
    teaspoon each of both light and dark soy sauce
4 tablespoons water
1 onion, sliced
1 large handful bean sprouts
Pinch of black pepper
Small pinch of white pepper
¼ teaspoon toasted sesame oil
1 spring onion, finely sliced to serve

Drop the egg noodles into boiling water and simmer for 2–3 minutes, stirring well to separate the noodles. Rinse thoroughly under cold water, drain and toss with the vegetable oil. Set aside.

In a small bowl, combine the soy sauce and water.

Heat a wok or frying pan to a high heat. Add a little vegetable oil. Add the onion and stir-fry for 2 minutes.

Add the bean sprouts and noodles. Add the soy sauce and water mixture, mix well and stir-fry over a high heat for a further 2 minutes or until the sauce begins to evaporate.

Add the black pepper and white pepper. Mix well. Add the toasted sesame oil and mix once again.

Pour the plain chow mein noodles into a long foil tray, garnish with the spring onion if desired and serve with any Chinese dish.

CRISPY SEAWEED
(Chinese Takeaway Style)

Serves 1

7–8 large cabbage, pak choi or spring green leaves
Oil for deep frying
½ teaspoon sugar
Pinch of salt

Remove the stalks from the cabbage or spring green leaves. Roll the leaves up and shred into fine strips.

Wash the leaves in cold water until clean. Pat dry with kitchen paper, arrange the leaves on a baking tray and place into a preheated oven at 150°C/300°F/Gas Mark 2 for around 12 minutes. Remove the leaves from the oven and set aside until ready for use. The dried leaves will keep well in a sealed container for up to 24 hours.

When ready to cook, heat the oil for deep-frying over a medium-high heat. When the oil is hot, carefully drop the leaves into the oil. Fry for around 30 seconds or until crisp.

Remove the leaves from the pan using a spider or slotted spoon. Drain off any excess oil and toss the leaves in the sugar and salt. Serve with any Chinese dish.

CHICKEN WINGS IN HOISIN SAUCE

(CHINESE TAKEAWAY STYLE)

Serves 1–2

4 tablespoons tomato ketchup
4 tablespoons hoisin sauce
4 tablespoons honey
1½ tablespoons soy sauce (recommended brand: Kikkoman)
2 teaspoons toasted sesame oil
1 teaspoon vegetable oil
Pinch of salt and pinch of black pepper
6 chicken wings, split into 12 wing pieces and tips discarded

In a large bowl, combine the tomato ketchup, hoisin sauce, honey, soy sauce and toasted sesame oil. Mix well and set aside.

In a separate bowl, combine the vegetable oil, salt, black pepper and chicken wing pieces. Mix well by hand and arrange the wings on a baking tray. Cover loosely with foil.

Preheat the oven to 180°C/350°F/Gas Mark 4.

Bake the wings for 30–40 minutes or until just cooked through. Remove the wings from the oven and set aside to cool slightly.

Heat a dry griddle pan to a low-medium heat. Add the chicken wings to the pan and cook for 7–8 minutes, basting occasionally with the prepared sauce. Turn the chicken pieces often to ensure even cooking and allow the sauce to caramelise.

When the wings are nicely charred, remove from the pan and arrange on a large plate. Serve as a starter to any Chinese meal, or simply as a snack.

POPCORN CHICKEN

(AMERICAN FAST-FOOD STYLE)

Serves 1–2

The ultimate in fried chicken, snack sized pieces with a mildly seasoned crispy coating.

10 tablespoons plain flour
5 tablespoons panko breadcrumbs (page 181)
Large pinch of salt
¼ teaspoon black pepper
1 teaspoon garlic powder
¼ teaspoon onion granules
Pinch of white pepper
Pinch of cayenne pepper
Pinch of Chinese 5-spice
Pinch of dried sage
¼ teaspoon paprika
¼ teaspoon dried oregano
¼ teaspoon dried Italian herbs
¼ teaspoon icing sugar
1 egg
120 ml/4 fl oz semi-skimmed milk
**2 large skinless, boneless chicken breast fillets (around 113 g/
    4 oz weight per fillet)**
Oil for deep frying

In a large bowl, combine the plain flour, panko breadcrumbs, salt, black pepper, garlic powder, onion granules, white pepper, cayenne pepper, Chinese 5-spice, sage, paprika, oregano, Italian herbs and icing sugar. Mix thoroughly and set aside.

In a separate bowl, combine the egg and milk. Whisk thoroughly.

Use scissors to cut the chicken into very small pieces. Keeping one hand dry, dip the chicken pieces first into the seasoned coating, then into the egg and milk mixture, and finally into the seasoned coating once again.

Leave to rest for a few minutes and repeat the process again if desired for a thicker coating.

Fry the popcorn chicken in small batches in hot oil on a medium heat for 2 minutes. Remove from the pan and rest for 2 minutes (the chicken will continue to cook on the inside). Finish the chicken by returning the pieces to the hot oil for a further minute or until the chicken is cooked through and the coating is crisp and golden.

Serve the popcorn chicken with a selection of dips.

BONELESS BUFFALO CHICKEN STRIPS

(AMERICAN FAST-FOOD STYLE)

Serves 1

Hot and fiery, these 'boneless wings' are the latest and spiciest addition to American fast-food menus.

4 tablespoons plain flour
6 tablespoons panko breadcrumbs (page 181)
¼ teaspoon garlic powder
¼ teaspoon onion powder
½ teaspoon dried Italian herbs
Pinch of black pepper
1 egg
120 ml/4 fl oz semi-skimmed milk
1 large skinless, boneless chicken breast fillet (around 113 g/ 4 oz weight)
Oil for deep frying
2 tablespoons hot pepper sauce (recommended brand: Frank's Red Hot Sauce)
2 tablespoons butter

Spread the plain flour over a plate. Set aside.

In a large bowl, combine the panko breadcrumbs, garlic powder, onion powder, dried Italian herbs and black pepper. Set aside.

In a small bowl, combine the egg and milk and mix thoroughly.

Trim any excess fat from the chicken breast and cut into 5–6 long strips.

Keeping one hand dry, dip the chicken strips first into the plain flour, then into the egg and milk mixture, and finally into the seasoned breadcrumbs.

Heat the oil over a medium-high heat. Carefully place the breaded chicken pieces into the oil and fry for 2 minutes.

Remove the chicken pieces from the pan and set aside on a plate for 1 minute. This will allow the chicken to continue cooking inside without overcooking the breaded coating.

Return the chicken pieces to the oil and fry for a further 2 minutes or until the breadcrumbs begin to turn golden and the chicken is cooked through. Remove the chicken strips from the pan and drain off any excess oil.

In a small pot, combine the hot pepper sauce and butter. Mix well until piping hot.

Place the cooked chicken strips into a sealable container. Add the hot pepper sauce/butter mixture. Close the lid and shake the container well until all of the chicken pieces are fully coated in the hot sauce.

Serve with celery, blue cheese dip (page 147) or coleslaw.

AMERICAN BARBECUE RIBS

(AMERICAN FAST-FOOD STYLE)

Serves 1–2

800 g/2 lb pork ribs
60 ml/2 fl oz water
2 tablespoons red wine vinegar
6 tablespoons tomato ketchup
6 tablespoons water
1½ tablespoons white wine vinegar
2 tablespoons Worcester sauce
1 tablespoon American mustard (recommended brand: French's)
1 tablespoon margarine
1 tablespoon treacle
½ teaspoon Tabasco sauce
Pinch of salt
1 teaspoon vegetable oil

Arrange the ribs on a large, deep roasting tray. In a small bowl, mix together the water and red wine vinegar. Pour the mixture over the pork ribs. Cover the roasting tray loosely with foil. Preheat the oven to 180°C/350°F/Gas Mark 4.

Bake the ribs for 40 minutes. Remove the ribs from the oven and arrange on a plate to cool. The ribs can be finished immediately, or refrigerated and finished the next day.

In a bowl, combine the tomato ketchup, water, white wine vinegar, Worcester sauce, American mustard, margarine, treacle, Tabasco sauce, salt and vegetable oil. Mix thoroughly.

Heat a dry griddle pan to a low-medium heat. Pour the cooked ribs into a large bowl and add 2 tablespoons of the prepared barbecue sauce. Mix thoroughly by hand.

Place the pork ribs onto the griddle pan. Baste with the remaining barbecue sauce every few minutes and cook the ribs, turning occasionally, for 10–12 minutes or until the sauce caramelises around the ribs. Serve with sweetcorn and coleslaw.

BARBECUE BEANS

(AMERICAN FAST-FOOD STYLE)

Serves 1–2

This recipe makes excellent use of tinned beans to create a deep BBQ flavour, perfect to serve with fried chicken dishes or as a side dish with tortilla chips.

1 teaspoon vegetable oil
1 small onion, sliced
1 teaspoon tomato purée
1 teaspoon yellow mustard (recommended brand: French's)
½ tablespoon black treacle
½ teaspoon Worcester sauce
Pinch of garlic powder
Pinch of paprika
3 tablespoons tomato ketchup
112 ml/4 fl oz vegetable stock, or 112 ml/4 fl oz water and
   ¼ vegetable stock cube
50 ml/2 fl oz water
1 teaspoon brown sugar
200 g/8 oz (half an average tin) baked beans in tomato sauce

Heat the oil in a pan over a low heat. Add the onion and tomato purée and stir-fry for 3–4 minutes or until the onion is golden.

Add the mustard, treacle, Worcester sauce, garlic powder, paprika, ketchup, stock, water and brown sugar. Simmer over a medium heat for 5–6 minutes or until thick.

Add the baked beans and mix thoroughly. Simmer for a further 2 minutes or until the beans are heated through.

Serve with popcorn chicken (page 140).

SALT AND SWEET POPCORN
(Cinema Style)

Serves 2

There is nothing like the smell of freshly made popcorn. This recipe satisfies both those with a savoury and with a sweet tooth. Made in minutes and amounting to only pennies per portion, it's the perfect snack for your home cinema nights.

4 tablespoons vegetable oil
8 tablespoons popping corn
2 tablespoons brown sugar
Salt to taste

Add the oil to a large pan with a lid (leave the lid off for now). Heat over a medium heat until almost smoking.

Stir in the popping corn and stir immediately to coat the corn with oil. As soon as the corn looks as though it's about to start popping, add the brown sugar and put the lid on.

Shake the pan constantly over the heat as the corn pops to ensure the sugar doesn't burn and is equally mixed with the popcorn. Keep shaking the pan until the popping slows down and all of the popping corn has popped.

Remove the pan from the heat and set aside for 1 minute. Pour the popcorn into a large container. Season to taste with salt and serve.

MINTED YOGURT DIP

(INDIAN RESTAURANT STYLE)

Serves 1

Fresh and cooling, this dip is perfect with any spicy kebab or curry.

3 tablespoons natural yogurt
⅓ teaspoon mint sauce
2 teaspoons smooth mango chutney
1 teaspoon white sugar
½ teaspoon lemon juice or lemon dressing

In a small bowl, combine the natural yogurt, mint sauce, mango chutney, sugar and lemon juice or lemon dressing.

Mix thoroughly and refrigerate for at least 1 hour before serving.

BLUE CHEESE DIP

(AMERICAN FAST-FOOD STYLE)

Serves 1–2

Around 50 g/2 oz Stilton cheese
75 ml/2½ fl oz sour cream
1 tablespoon mayonnaise (recommended brand: Hellman's)
1 teaspoon lemon juice
Pinch of salt and pinch of black pepper

In a large bowl, combine the Stilton, sour cream and mayonnaise. Mix thoroughly until soft and smooth.

Add the lemon juice, salt and pepper. Mix thoroughly once more. Chill the blue cheese dip in the fridge for at least 2 hours before serving with boneless buffalo chicken strips (page 142).

SOUR CREAM AND CHIVE DIP
(AMERICAN FAST-FOOD STYLE)

Serves 1–2

This cooling dip is perfect during summer weather, adding a refreshing angle to baked potatoes or any barbecue food.

4 tablespoons sour cream
4 tablespoons soft cheese
1 garlic clove, crushed
Around 1 tablespoon of fresh chives, snipped fine with scissors
Pinch of salt
Pinch of paprika or cayenne pepper (optional)

In a bowl, combine the sour cream, soft cheese, crushed garlic, fresh chives and salt. Add the paprika or cayenne pepper if desired.

Mix thoroughly and refrigerate for at least 1 hour before serving with tortilla chips, breadsticks or fresh vegetables.

CHIPPY SAUCE
(CHIP SHOP STYLE)

Makes around 200 ml/7 fl oz of sauce

In the east of Scotland, 'salt 'n' sauce' is the preferred topping to any chip shop dish. The thin, tangy brown sauce has become famous through the years and can often be found on chip shop counters, poured into old Irn-Bru bottles for use by the customer! The debate on which watering down method should be used is fierce – many people argue that the sauce should be thinned down with vinegar as opposed to water. Of course, vinegar costs money while tap water is free! Feel free to try both variations on the sauce and I hope you'll agree that water is the true necessary ingredient.

180 ml/6 fl oz bottle 'gold star' brown sauce
30 ml/1½ fl oz water (or vinegar if desired)

Mix the brown sauce and water thoroughly. Serve with chips or any chip shop dish. The sauce will keep well in the fridge for several days.

GARLIC AND HERB DIP

(AMERICAN FAST-FOOD STYLE)

Serves 1

2 tablespoons mayonnaise (recommended brand: Hellman's)
½ teaspoon American mustard (recommended brand: French's)
¼ teaspoon garlic powder
¼ teaspoon dried parsley
2–3 tablespoons semi-skimmed milk

In a small bowl, combine the mayonnaise, American mustard, garlic powder and dried parsley. Mix well. Slowly add the semi-skimmed milk until the sauce reaches the desired consistency. Serve with pizzas and kebabs.

HOUSE SPECIAL CHILLI SAUCE

(KEBAB SHOP STYLE)

Serves 3–4

Perfect with kebabs and pakoras. Inexpensive 'economy' supermarket varieties of ketchup will work well in the finished sauce. The flavour of the sauce will improve overnight making it ideal to prepare in advance.

200 ml/7 fl oz tomato ketchup
1 teaspoon mint sauce
75–100 ml/2½–3½ fl oz water
1 large tomato, chopped
1 small onion, chopped
1 red pepper, chopped
½ teaspoon chilli powder
½ teaspoon salt
5 tablespoons tinned mixed fruit cocktail

In a blender, combine the tomato ketchup, mint sauce, 75 ml/2½ fl oz of the water, tomato, onion, red pepper, chilli powder, salt and fruit cocktail.

Blend thoroughly until the sauce becomes smooth. Add the remaining water if necessary until the sauce reaches the desired consistency. Pour the sauce into dip trays and set aside in the fridge for at least 2 hours before serving.

FRESH SALSA

(Mexican Style)

Serves 1–2

This simple salsa is delicious added to nachos, or can be used as a dip with kebabs and pakoras.

1 large tomato
½ red onion, finely chopped
½ red pepper, finely chopped
½ green pepper, finely chopped
1 finger chilli pepper, finely sliced (see page 62)
1 garlic clove, crushed
¼ teaspoon dried parsley
¼ teaspoon salt
Pinch of black pepper
1 tablespoon olive oil
2 teaspoons lime juice

Quarter the tomato and remove the seeds. Finely chop the tomato flesh and place it in a large bowl.

Add the red onion, red pepper, green pepper, chilli and garlic. Mix thoroughly.

Add the dried parsley, salt, black pepper, olive oil and lime juice. Mix thoroughly once again and refrigerate for at least 1 hour before serving.

Serve with pollo fritto, or with any Mexican dish.

LOADED JALAPENO NACHOS
(MEXICAN STYLE)

Serves 1

1 tablespoon butter
1 tablespoon plain flour
120 ml/4 fl oz semi-skimmed milk
4 processed cheese slices
Pinch of salt
1 large handful tortilla chips
3 tablespoons fresh salsa (see opposite)
2 tablespoons jarred jalapeno peppers

In a small pot over a low heat, melt the butter and add the plain flour. Mix well.

Add the semi-skimmed milk and stir until the mixture is combined. Simmer for 1–2 minutes, stirring constantly.

Add the processed cheese slices and mix well. Simmer for a further 5 minutes or until the sauce becomes bright yellow and thickens. Add a little extra milk if the mixture becomes too thick and continue simmering for longer if the mixture is too thin.

Season the sauce with a pinch of salt, mix well and set aside.

Arrange the tortilla chips on a large plate. Scatter the fresh salsa over the chips.

Pat the jalapeno peppers dry with kitchen paper. Scatter the jalapenos over the tortilla chips. Add 3–4 tablespoons of the cheese sauce over the chips.

Microwave the loaded nachos for 30–40 seconds on full heat until piping hot. Remove the plate from the microwave, allow to cool for 1 minute and serve.

If desired, additional toppings may be added to the nachos including refried beans, chilli con carne and sour cream.

9

BREAKFAST AND LUNCH

While takeaway and fast foods are the perfect treat for weekends and busy days, many of us also spend vast amounts of money on everyday dishes, particularly if we require a good meal to start the working day or to keep us going from lunch through the afternoon. Bakeries, delis and even supermarkets now offer a wide range of sandwiches, soups and snacks designed to keep hunger at bay for busy workers. While this undoubtedly offers great convenience, the cost of these dishes can quickly add up until it takes a considerable chunk out of the monthly wage.

Preparing these dishes at home offers the perfect alternative, especially when those breakfast and lunch items can be assembled the night before and taken to work the next day. The end result is more take-home pay and more time spent enjoying lunch during a well-earned break with no need to spend time in queues in order to purchase your meals.

SUMMER FRUITS MUFFINS

(AMERICAN FAST-FOOD STYLE)

Serves 6–8 large muffins

Packed with healthy fruit and perfect for freezing. Do not defrost the frozen fruits before use or they will become too wet.

200 g/7 oz plain flour
Large pinch of salt
2 teaspoons baking powder
100 g/3½ oz caster sugar
140 g/5 oz frozen summer fruits
1 egg
3 tablespoons margarine, melted
Around 100 ml/3½ fl oz semi-skimmed milk

Preheat the oven to 200°C/400°F/Gas Mark 6.

In a large bowl, combine the plain flour, salt, baking powder, sugar and mixed fruits. Mix well.

In a separate bowl, combine the egg, melted margarine and semi-skimmed milk. Mix well and add to the dry ingredients.

Fold the wet and dry ingredients together until just mixed.

Pour a large tablespoon of the mixture into each muffin tray. Bake the muffins for around 25 minutes. Check that the muffins are completely cooked by piercing the centre of a muffin with a fork. The muffins are ready when the fork comes out clean.

Remove the muffins from the oven and leave to rest for 5 minutes before removing from the tray and arranging on a wire rack to cool completely.

The muffins will freeze well for up to 1 month.

BACON, CHEESE AND FOLDED-EGG OMELETTE BAGEL

(AMERICAN FAST-FOOD STYLE)

Serves 1

In recent years, American fast-food restaurants have expanded breakfast menus considerably. This bagel is the perfect start to the day and can be recreated faithfully using the ingredients listed.

1 bagel (recommended brand: New York Bakery Co)
2 teaspoons margarine
2 processed cheese slices
2 slices lean bacon
1 egg
2 tablespoons semi-skimmed milk
½ teaspoon vegetable oil
Pinch of salt and pinch of black pepper

Preheat a grill to a medium-high heat.

Slice the bagel in two. Arrange the bagel on a wire rack and toast under the hot grill for around 2 minutes, or until toasted and golden.

Arrange the bagel halves on a sheet of foil.

Spread one teaspoon of margarine onto each bagel half and place a processed cheese slice on top of each.

Arrange the bacon on the wire rack and grill for around 5–6 minutes or until cooked through, turning once. Place the cooked bacon on top of one bagel half.

In a small bowl, combine the egg and semi-skimmed milk. Whisk thoroughly.

Heat a non-stick wok or frying pan over a high heat. Add the vegetable oil. Pour half of the egg/milk mixture into the pan. Add salt and pepper. Tilt the pan if necessary in order to let any uncooked egg/milk move around the pan and cook.

Carefully slide a thin spatula underneath the cooked egg mixture and shake the pan forcefully until the egg omelette moves freely around the pan. Use the spatula to flip the egg or, if feeling brave, toss the egg in the pan. Allow the other side of the omelette to cook for a further 20–30 seconds and remove onto a plate. Repeat the process with the remaining egg mixture if desired.

Fold the egg omelette twice and place it on top of the bacon. Complete the bagel by adding the remaining cheese topped bagel half.

Wrap the bagel loosely in foil or baking paper and place in the oven at the lowest available setting for 3–4 minutes to combine flavours and heat through. Serve with mini hash browns (see overleaf).

MINI HASH BROWNS

(AMERICAN FAST-FOOD STYLE)

Serves 2–3 (makes about 42 mini hash browns)

These crispy potato bites are the perfect breakfast side dish. American fast-food chains use specially designed machine moulds in order to create their hash browns. This recipe recreates that machinery using simple ice-cube trays!

4 large potatoes
1 teaspoon butter
1 teaspoon salt
Large pinch of black pepper
¾ teaspoon white sugar
1 egg
6 tablespoons plain flour
Oil for deep frying

Peel the potatoes and place in a large pan of water. Add a pinch of salt and bring to the boil. Allow the potatoes to boil for around 5–6 minutes. Drain and set aside.

When the potatoes have cooled to room temperature, place them in a food-safe bag and refrigerate for 1 hour until cold.

Grate the potatoes into a large bowl. Add the butter, salt, black pepper, white sugar, egg and plain flour. Mix thoroughly. The mixture should become very sticky.

Use two teaspoons to drop the mixture into ice-cube trays. Freeze the potato mixture overnight.

Heat some oil for deep-frying to a medium-high heat. Carefully push the frozen mini hash browns out of their ice cube trays and into a large bowl.

Cook the hash browns in batches. Place the mini hash browns into the hot oil. Fry for around 3 minutes. Remove the hash browns and set aside on a plate for 2 minutes. This will allow the potato to continue cooking on the inside without too much browning.

Return the mini hash browns to the oil and fry for a further 2–3 minutes or until golden, crispy and cooked through.

Remove the hash browns from the pan, drain off any excess oil and serve with bacon, cheese and folded egg omelette bagels.

STRAWBERRY SMOOTHIE

(American Fast-Food Style)

Serves 1–2

200 ml/7 fl oz semi-skimmed milk
100 ml/3½ fl oz low fat vanilla yogurt
140 g/5 oz frozen strawberries
4–6 ice cubes

In a blender, combine the semi-skimmed milk, vanilla yogurt, frozen strawberries and ice cubes.

Blend thoroughly for 1 minute or until completely smooth before serving.

BREAKFAST BURRITO

(AMERICAN FAST-FOOD STYLE)

Serves 1

Roughly 56 g/2 oz pork mince
Pinch of salt
Pinch of black pepper
Pinch of white sugar
1 egg mixed with 2 tablespoons semi-skimmed milk
1 large flour tortilla wrap
1 processed cheese slice
2 tablespoons fresh salsa (page 150)

In a small bowl, combine the pork mince, salt, black pepper and sugar. Mix well.

Heat a little vegetable oil in a pan over a high heat. Add the prepared pork mixture to the pan and stir-fry for 3–4 minutes or until the mince is cooked through. Remove the mince from the pan, drain off any excess oil and set aside.

Add a touch more vegetable oil to the pan. Pour the egg mixture into the pan and allow to set briefly. Stir-fry the eggs over a medium-high heat until scrambled. Add salt and pepper to taste.

Return the cooked pork mince to the pan and stir-fry with the eggs for a further minute.

Heat a dry, flat frying pan over a medium-high heat. Place the tortilla wrap into the pan and cook over a high heat for 30–40 seconds, turning frequently until warmed through.

Place the processed cheese slice onto the middle of the warmed tortilla wrap. Add the fresh salsa. Pour the pork and egg mixture on top, wrap and serve.

TUNA PASTA SALAD
(Deli/Bakery Style)

Serves 2–3

Pinch of salt
100 g/3½ oz pasta shells
½ teaspoon olive oil
1 x 190 g/7 oz tin tuna in springwater, drained
1 teaspoon lemon juice or lemon dressing
Pinch of salt
½ small red onion, finely sliced
½ red pepper, finely sliced
½ green pepper, finely sliced
1 tomato, deseeded and chopped
⅛ cucumber, deseeded and chopped
4 tablespoons tinned sweetcorn, drained
4 tablespoons (or to taste) mayonnaise (recommended brand:
   Hellman's)
Pinch of black pepper
Pinch of dried parsley

Fill a large pot with water and add a pinch of salt. Bring to the boil, add
the pasta shells and stir once. Boil the pasta according to packet
instructions until soft with just a little bite (or 'al dente'). Rinse briefly
with cold water, drain thoroughly and toss with the olive oil.

In a large bowl, combine the tuna, lemon juice or lemon dressing and
pinch of salt. Mix thoroughly. Add the red onion, red pepper, green
pepper, tomato, cucumber and tinned sweetcorn. Mix thoroughly.

Add the mayonnaise and mix thoroughly again. Season to taste with salt
and black pepper, add the dried parsley and mix a final time.

Refrigerate the tuna pasta salad for at least 1 hour. Remove from the
fridge 20 minutes before use and serve with shredded iceberg lettuce if
desired. Add the lettuce just before use in order to ensure it stays crisp.

The pasta salad will keep well in the fridge for up to 2 days.

PASTRY STEAK
(Deli/Bakery Style)

Recipe makes enough filling for 3–4 pastry steaks

This hugely popular bakery snack is an excellent use of leftover stews and casseroles. The prepared stew may be frozen in portions for up to 3 months.

2 teaspoons vegetable oil
2 large carrots, chopped
½ baby turnip (around 200 g/7 oz), chopped
1 large onion, chopped
500 g/1.1 lb braising steak, diced
Pinch of salt
2 tablespoons plain flour
1 tablespoon tomato purée
2 teaspoons Worcester sauce
450 ml/16 fl oz beef stock (or 450 ml/16 fl oz boiling water
**   mixed with 1 beef stock cube)**
1 teaspoon dried mixed herbs
1 teaspoon dried parsley
Pinch of black pepper
100 g/3½ oz puff pastry per pastry steak (uncooked weight)
1 egg, beaten

Heat 1 teaspoon of vegetable oil in a large pot over a low-medium heat. Add the carrots, turnip and onion. Stir-fry for 5–6 minutes.

In a large bowl, combine the braising steak, salt and flour. Heat the remaining teaspoon of oil in a frying pan over a high heat and brown the diced steak for 1–2 minutes.

Add the browned beef to the vegetables. Add the tomato purée and Worcester sauce. Cook for a further 3–4 minutes.

Add the beef stock, mixed herbs, parsley and black pepper. Bring to the boil, reduce the heat to low and cover with a tight fitting lid. Simmer for 1½–2 hours. Add a little extra water during cooking if necessary.

When the stew has cooked, remove the vegetables and eat or discard. Remove the beef pieces from the pan and set aside to cool. Shred the beef into tiny pieces and mix with the remaining gravy. The beef and gravy mixture may now be stored in 3–4 tablespoon amounts for use in future pastry steaks.

Roll out 100 g/3½ oz of puff pastry to a large square, roughly 15 x 15 cm (6 x 6 inches). Add 3–4 tablespoons of beef and gravy mixture to one half of the pastry. Fold the remaining pastry over the mixture. Press the dough down firmly to ensure a seal is created. Use a fork to create a crimped edge effect if desired.

Place the pastry steak on a baking tray and brush with beaten egg. Pierce the pastry steak in the centre with a knife in order to allow steam to escape during cooking.

Preheat the oven to 220°C/425°F/ Gas Mark 7.

Bake the pastry steak for 25 minutes or until the pastry is golden and cooked through and the filling is piping hot. Remove from the oven and stand for 3–4 minutes before serving.

BLT SALAD

(Deli/Bakery Style)

Serves 1–2

This bacon salad is becoming increasingly popular and has its origins in the classic BLT sandwich.

3 slices wholemeal brown bread
4 slices smoked bacon
1 tomato
1 small handful shredded iceberg lettuce
2 tablespoons mayonnaise
Pinch of black pepper

Preheat a grill on a medium-high setting.

Toast the bread slices under the grill for 2–3 minutes on each side or until golden. Set aside to cool.

Place the bacon on a tray and place under the grill for 2–3 minutes on each side or until just crisp and cooked through. Cool slightly and cut into small pieces.

Quarter the tomato and use a knife to remove the seeds. Chop the tomato into small pieces.

Cut the toasted bread into small croûtons. Place in a large bowl with the bacon pieces, tomato and shredded lettuce.

Add the mayonnaise and black pepper. Mix well and serve.

SAUSAGE ROLLS

(DELI/BAKERY STYLE)

Makes 5 large sausage rolls

Any good brand of sausages will work well in this dish, simply cut the sausages open and remove the meat before combining with the remaining ingredients.

500 g/1.1 lb sausage meat or sausages, skinned
2 tinned plum tomatoes
1 onion, finely chopped
Pinch of dried mixed herbs
Pinch of salt
Pinch of black pepper
1 egg
500 g/1.1 lb puff pastry

In a large bowl, combine the sausage meat or sausages, plum tomatoes, chopped onion, herbs, salt and black pepper. Mix well by hand until all of the ingredients are well combined.

Whisk the egg in a bowl and set aside.

Divide the dough into 5 equal pieces. Roll out one piece of pastry to a large square, around 15 x15 cm (6 x 6 inches) in size.

Add 2–3 tablespoons of the sausage roll filling onto one half of the pastry strip. Brush the edge of the pastry with beaten egg and fold over the filling. Press down and pinch the dough to form a seal. Crimp with a fork if desired. Repeat the process with the remaining pastry and filling. Brush each sausage roll with beaten egg.

Preheat the oven to 200°C/400°F/Gas Mark 6. Place the sausage rolls onto a baking tray and cook for around 20 minutes or until the pastry is golden and the filling is cooked through.

Remove the sausage rolls from the oven and set aside to cool for 5 minutes before serving.

ULTIMATE CHEESE TOASTIE
(DELI/BAKERY STYLE)

Serves 1

Delicious pan-fried toasties made with minimum effort and little mess.

2 slices white bread
2 teaspoons margarine
3–4 thick slices Cheddar cheese

Butter each slice of bread with 1 teaspoon of margarine. Place the buttered bread slices together as if to make a sandwich with no filling. Arrange the cheese slices across the top bread slice. Heat a non-stick frying pan over a medium heat. When the pan is hot, lift the cheese topped slice of bread and place it butter side down in the pan. Add the remaining bread slice, butter side up. Press down gently on the bread with a spatula. As the toastie cooks, the cheese will melt and hold the bread together.

Cook the toastie for around 2–3 minutes over a medium heat. Using the spatula, flip the toastie over and continue to cook for a further 2–3 minutes on the other side, or until the cheese is fully melted and the bread is golden and crisp. Remove the toastie from the pan and serve with tomato soup.

TOMATO SOUP
(DELI/BAKERY STYLE)

Makes enough soup for 3 portions

2 tablespoons olive oil
1 medium onion, finely chopped
1 garlic clove, crushed
1½ tablespoons tomato purée
2 x 400 g/14 oz tins of peeled plum tomatoes
Dash of Worcester sauce (optional)
1 small handful fresh basil leaves OR ¼ teaspoon dried Italian herbs
Pinch of sugar
Pinch of salt and pinch of black pepper
Pinch of bicarbonate of soda and 200 ml/7 fl oz semi-skimmed milk per portion to serve

Heat the olive oil in a large pot over a low heat. Add the chopped onion and crushed garlic. Stir-fry for 1 minute.

Add the tomato purée and continue to stir-fry for 3–4 minutes.

Add the tinned tomatoes, Worcester sauce (if desired), fresh basil or dried Italian herbs, sugar, salt and black pepper. Mix well and bring to the boil. Once boiling, reduce the heat to low and simmer for 20 minutes until the tomatoes start to thicken.

Pour the tomatoes into a blender and blitz until smooth. For an even smoother soup, press the mixture through a sieve.

Divide the tomato mixture into 3 equal portions of around 200 ml/ 7 fl oz. Each portion can be finished individually now or frozen for up to 1 month before finishing as below. Each 200 ml/7 fl oz portion of tomato soup base should be finished with 200 ml/7 fl oz of milk.

To finish the soup, add 1 portion of tomato soup base to a pot over a low heat. In a small bowl, combine the bicarbonate of soda and 2 tablespoons of milk. Mix well and add to the pot.

Add 200 ml/7 fl oz of semi-skimmed milk. Bring to boiling point, reduce the heat to low and simmer for 5–6 minutes. The mixture will fizz a little as the bicarbonate of soda combines with the acidic tomatoes. This is normal and the soup should become smooth after simmering.

Serve the tomato soup with the ultimate cheese toastie.

10

DESSERTS

What better way to round off the meal than with a delicious and indulgent dessert? Takeaway menus offer various treats such as cookies, cakes and ice cream, unfortunately often highly priced but irresistible. Preparing your own desserts at home keeps the cost down. However, the temptation remains the same so self-control must be exercised nonetheless!

Many people feel apprehensive about cooking desserts in comparison to savoury foods as they believe that everything must be weighed out precisely, mixed in a particular order and baked for not a minute longer than required! However, even a novice can create some delicious cakes and biscuits with just a little know-how. Following a few simple tips will make sure that everything goes to plan.

When recipes call for butter or margarine, the classic ingredient 'Stork' is highly recommended. Less expensive than premium butters, it's the spread of choice in many bakeries and will deliver excellent results in cakes and biscuits. Equally, while expensive or high cocoa content chocolate may be used if desired, inexpensive brands will also offer very good results so feel free to make your ingredient choice based on budget and availability.

Most of the desserts included here can be prepared in advance, making it easy to ensure that a range of treats is available for both you and your guests. Many of the desserts can be frozen, making life easier still and allowing your chocolate fudge cake to be rationed out over the course of a few weeks as opposed to a few days. That's the theory, although this is of course very much dependent on willpower!

APPLE PIE SLICES

(AMERICAN FAST-FOOD STYLE)

Serves 2

If serving immediately, warn your guests that the filling will be very hot!

3 apples
1½ tablespoons white sugar
1 tablespoon brown sugar
Pinch of cinnamon
Dash of lemon juice
2 tablespoons water
½ teaspoon cornflour mixed with 1 tablespoon water
120 g/4 oz plain flour
Small pinch of salt
4 tablespoons butter (or just under 60 g/2 oz)
Around 50 ml/2 fl oz water
2 teaspoons caster sugar to serve

Peel the apples and cut into small dice. Place in a small saucepan and add both lots of sugar, the cinnamon, lemon juice and water. Mix well. Cook the apples over a low heat for 8–10 minutes or until soft, stirring often. When the apples have softened, add the cornflour and water mixture, mix well once again and simmer for a further 2 minutes. Mash the apple mixture well and set aside to cool.

In a large bowl, combine the plain flour and salt. Mix well. Add the butter and mix well into the flour until well combined. Add the water and stir until the dough is formed. Empty on to a floured work surface and roll out thinly.

Cut 2 rectangular strips from the dough, around 15 x 15 cm/6 x 6 inches in size. Heap the apple mixture onto one side of both pastry strips. Try to leave the edges free of filling. Use a little water to moisten the other half of each pastry strip and fold over on top of the filling. Pinch the dough well until fully sealed, or use a fork to create a crimped effect.

Fry the apple pie slices in hot oil over a medium heat for 2–3 minutes per side or until golden. Remove from the pan and drain off any excess oil.

Sprinkle the apple pie slices with caster sugar and serve immediately or cool to room temperature.

CHURROS WITH CHOCOLATE CREAM SAUCE

(MEXICAN/SPANISH RESTAURANT STYLE)

Serves 2–3

Also known as 'Spanish Doughnuts' (although often sold in Mexican restaurants), these sweet fried pastries are best eaten warm.

200 ml/7 fl oz water
1 tablespoon vegetable oil
Pinch of salt
1 teaspoon caster sugar
120 g/4 oz plain flour
Pinch of baking powder
Oil for deep frying
2 tablespoons caster sugar mixed with a pinch of cinnamon
powder
2 tablespoons chocolate and hazelnut spread (recommended
brand: Nutella)
1 tablespoon double cream
4 tablespoons semi-skimmed milk

In a small pot, combine the water, vegetable oil, salt and caster sugar. Bring to the boil.

Once boiling, remove from the heat. Combine the flour and baking powder and mix well. Slowly add the flour mixture to the liquid, whisking thoroughly until a smooth, thick dough/batter is created. Set aside for 10 minutes.

Put the batter mixture into a piping bag with a star-shaped nozzle.

Heat the oil over a medium heat. Once hot, carefully pipe several long strips of batter into the hot oil. Fry the churros for around 2–3 minutes per side or until cooked through and golden.

If a piping bag is not available, the churros can be shaped by hand. Take a small handful of the batter mixture and roll it between your hands into a long, thin sausage shape. Repeat this process until all the batter is used and fry as above.

Remove the cooked churros from the pan and drain off any excess oil. Roll the churros in the caster sugar/cinnamon mix.

In a small pot, combine the chocolate and hazelnut spread, double cream and semi-skimmed milk. Mix thoroughly over a low heat and simmer for 3–4 minutes or until the sauce thickens slightly.

Arrange the churros on a plate and serve with the chocolate cream sauce on the side.

CHOCOLATE FUDGE CAKE

(AMERICAN FAST-FOOD STYLE)

Makes 1 large cake

300 g/10½ oz plain flour
50 g/2 oz cocoa powder
1 teaspoon bicarbonate of soda
1 teaspoon salt
125 g/4½ oz butter
300 g/10½ oz caster sugar
2 eggs
1 teaspoon vanilla extract
3 teaspoons white vinegar
Around 200 ml/7 fl oz semi-skimmed milk

Chocolate Butter Icing:
75 g/2½ oz unsalted butter
175 g/6 oz icing sugar
3–4 tablespoons cocoa powder
Semi-skimmed milk

Preheat the oven to 180°C/350°F/Gas Mark 4.

In a large bowl, sieve the plain flour, cocoa powder, bicarbonate of soda and salt. Mix thoroughly.

In a separate large bowl, cream the butter and caster sugar until fluffy. Add the eggs and vanilla extract and mix thoroughly.

Add the wet ingredients to the dry ingredients and whisk thoroughly. Add the vinegar and mix again. Add the milk and whisk until smooth.

Divide the mixture between two large round non-stick cake tins. Bake for around 20 minutes or until a fork inserted into the cake comes out clean.

Remove the cake tins from the oven and set aside to cool for 8–10 minutes. Remove the cakes from the tins and arrange on a wire rack to cool completely.

Make the chocolate butter icing by combining the unsalted butter, icing sugar and cocoa powder in a large bowl. Mix thoroughly, slowly adding semi-skimmed milk a tablespoon at a time until a medium thick spread is created.

Spread the chocolate butter cream over one half of the cake. Add the top half of the cake and spread with the remaining butter cream mixture.

Cut the cake into slices and serve. Individual slices will freeze well in small foil containers for up to 1 month.

If desired, heat the cake slices in a microwave for 15 seconds until just warm and serve with vanilla ice cream.

CHOCOLATE BROWNIES

(American Fast-Food Style)

Makes 12 brownies

250 g/8 oz dark chocolate
250 g/8 oz vegetable oil spread (recommended brand: Stork)
350 g/12 oz caster sugar
4 large eggs, lightly whisked
1 teaspoon vanilla extract
200 g/7 oz plain flour
1½ teaspoons baking powder
150 g/5 oz white, dark or milk chocolate, broken into pieces
(use any kind you prefer)

Break up the chocolate into pieces and add it to a pot over a very low heat. Stir the chocolate frequently and remove from the heat just before fully melted so that the residual heat finishes melting the chocolate. Set aside to cool slightly.

In a large bowl, cream together the vegetable oil spread and sugar until thoroughly combined. Add the eggs and vanilla extract. Add the melted chocolate, ensuring that it has sufficiently cooled so that it doesn't scramble the eggs. Add the plain flour and baking powder and mix until the flour is combined. Finally, add the broken chocolate pieces and mix lightly a final time.

Line a large cake tin with baking paper. Preheat the oven to 190°C/fan 170°C/375°F/Gas Mark 5.

Pour the brownie mix into the lined cake tin. Place the tin into the preheated oven on the middle shelf and bake for 40–50 minutes. To check the brownies, gently shake the cake tin from side to side. If the mixture is wobbly, return it to the oven for another few minutes.

Remove the cake tin from the oven and allow to cool for 5 minutes. Remove the brownie from the cake tin and peel off any baking paper while still warm in order to prevent it from sticking. Place the brownie on a wire rack and allow to cool completely. Cut the brownie into 12 large squares and serve.

CHOCOLATE AND BANANA CUPCAKES

(Deli/Bakery Style)

Makes 12 large cupcakes

75 g/2½ oz dark chocolate
2 medium bananas
100 g/3½ oz vegetable oil spread (recommended brand:
    Stork)
125 g/4½ oz golden caster sugar
1 teaspoon vanilla extract
3 eggs
50 g/2 oz cocoa powder
125 g/4½ oz plain flour
2 teaspoons baking powder

Preheat the oven to 180°C/350°F/Gas Mark 4. Break up the chocolate into pieces and add it to a pot over a very low heat. Stir the chocolate frequently and remove from the heat just before fully melted so that the residual heat finishes melting the chocolate.

Peel and mash the bananas and combine with the melted chocolate. Set aside.

In a large bowl, combine the vegetable oil spread, caster sugar and vanilla extract. Mix well. Add the eggs and whisk thoroughly into the mixture. The mixture will be very runny at this stage.

Add the cocoa powder and half of the flour. Stir well until fully combined. Add the remaining flour and baking powder and mix well once again.

Add the prepared chocolate and banana mixture to the bowl and stir just until a smooth batter is created.

Divide the mixture between 12 large muffin cases in a muffin tin. Fill each case around three-quarters full.

Bake in the oven for around 15 minutes, or until a fork inserted into the cupcakes comes out clean. Remove the cupcakes from the oven and leave for 5 minutes. Remove the cupcakes from the tray, arrange on a wire rack to cool completely and serve.

STICKY TOFFEE PUDDING

(DELI/BAKERY STYLE)

Makes 1 large sticky toffee pudding

150 g/5 oz dried and stoned dates
250 ml/9 fl oz weak black tea
½ teaspoon bicarbonate of soda
200 g/7 oz golden caster sugar
2 eggs, whisked
100 g/3½ oz vegetable oil spread (recommended brand: Stork)
200 g/7 oz self raising flour
1 teaspoon mixed spice
1 teaspoon vanilla extract
200 ml/7 fl oz double cream
1 x 397 g/14 oz tin of Dulce du Leche (milk based caramel sauce)

Preheat the oven to 180°C/350°F/Gas Mark 4.

Chop the dates and place them in a large pan over a medium heat. Add the tea and simmer for 2–3 minutes or until softened.

Reduce the heat to low and add the bicarbonate of soda. The mixture will become fizzy. Don't panic; this is what we want to happen! Switch off the heat, stir once and set aside.

In a large bowl, combine the sugar, eggs and vegetable oil spread. Mix well. Add half of the self raising flour and mix until fully incorporated into the mixture. Add the remaining flour, mixed spice and vanilla extract and mix thoroughly again.

Add the dates to the mix. If a smoother texture is desired, press the date mixture through a sieve before adding to the mix.

Pour the mixture into a greased cake tin (25 x 25 cm/10 x 10 inches) and bake in the oven for 35–40 minutes or until a skewer pierced into the mixture comes out clean. Remove the cake tin from the oven and set aside to cool for 5 minutes.

Remove the pudding from the cake tin and set on a wire rack. The pudding may be served straight away or cooled completely and reheated briefly in the microwave or oven before serving.

Pour the double cream and Dulce du Leche into a saucepan and warm gently over a low heat, stirring frequently until a smooth sauce is created. The prepared sauce will keep well in the fridge for several days if desired.

Place a portion of the sticky toffee pudding in a large bowl and pour over the prepared sauce. Serve with ice cream or custard.

ICE CREAM FRENZY
(AMERICAN FAST-FOOD STYLE)

Serves 1

This milk and ice cream mixture creates a soft, smooth ice cream in a similar way to that used in American fast-food restaurants.

20 g/1 oz of your favourite chocolate bar (around half a bar – dairy milk, flake or cream egg recommended)
200 g/7 oz vanilla ice cream
1–2 tablespoons semi-skimmed milk
1 tablespoon chocolate syrup (optional) (recommended brand: Tate and Lyle)

Place the chocolate bar in a food-safe bag and bash with a rolling pin until broken into medium sized pieces. Set aside.

Place the vanilla ice cream in a blender. Add the semi-skimmed milk and pulse in the blender until combined with the ice cream. The milk should help create a softer ice cream. Add a little more milk if necessary but be careful not to add too much or the ice cream will become too thin.

Scoop the softened ice cream out of the blender and into a serving cup or bowl. Add the chopped chocolate pieces and mix once. Serve topped with chocolate syrup if desired.

EMPIRE BISCUITS

(DELI/BAKERY STYLE)

Makes 12–15 Empire biscuits

Also known as 'double biscuits', these are a bakery classic.

200 g/7 fl oz vegetable oil spread (recommended brand: Stork)
125 g/4½ oz caster sugar
1 egg yolk
2 teaspoons vanilla extract
275 g/10 oz plain flour
2 tablespoons raspberry jam
2 tablespoons raspberry dessert sauce
Icing sugar
Water
15 jelly tot sweets or glacé cherries

Preheat the oven to 180°C/350°F/Gas Mark 4.

In a large bowl, combine the vegetable oil spread, sugar, egg yolk and vanilla extract. Mix well.

Slowly add the flour and mix well until dough is formed. All of the flour may not be needed. Use your hands to press the mixture together and knead until the dough becomes smooth. If the mixture is too crumbly, add a little more vegetable oil spread and knead again. Once the dough comes together, stop kneading so that the heat from your hands does not melt the spread.

Roll out the dough on a floured work surface to a thickness of around 5–7.5 mm (¼ inch). Cut circles out of the dough using a mug or cutter and place the rounds on a lightly greased baking tray.

Place the tray in the preheated oven and bake for around 10 minutes or until the biscuits are golden brown. The biscuits may seem soft when removed from the oven but will harden as they cool. Use a spatula to lift the biscuits on to a wire rack and set aside to cool completely.

In a small bowl, combine the raspberry jam and raspberry dessert sauce. Add 1–2 teaspoons of the mixture to half of the cooled biscuits and place the remaining biscuit halves on top to form a biscuit sandwich.

Spread 1 tablespoon of icing over the top of each biscuit. Top with a jelly tot sweet or glacé cherry and serve. The biscuits will keep well for 2 days in a sealed container.

AMBASSADOR'S CHOCOLATES
(Deli/Bakery Style)

Makes 4–6 chocolates

With these crispy, nutty chocolates you'll really spoil yourself and your guests!

3 crispbreads (recommended brand: Ryvita)
2 tablespoons chocolate and hazelnut spread (recommended brand: Nutella)

Crush the crispbreads in a blender or with a rolling pin.

Gently warm the chocolate and hazelnut spread in the microwave for a few seconds.

Pour the blended crispbreads into a mug and add the chocolate and hazelnut spread. Mix thoroughly.

Spoon the mixture into 4–6 cake cases and refrigerate for 2 hours or until set before serving.

WARM COOKIE DOUGH

(American Fast-Food Style)

Makes 4 portions of warm cookie dough

Crispy on the outside, soft and chewy in the middle, this warm dessert has become a hugely popular addition to pizza restaurant menus.

125 g/4 oz butter
100 g/3½ oz caster sugar
100 g/3½ oz brown sugar
1 egg
1 teaspoon vanilla extract
175 g/6 oz self raising flour
½ teaspoon salt
50 g/2 oz cocoa powder
100 g/3½ oz white chocolate chips

In a large bowl, combine the butter, caster sugar and brown sugar. Add the egg and vanilla extract and mix thoroughly once more.

Add the flour, salt, cocoa powder and white chocolate chips. Mix well until the dough comes together.

Preheat the oven to 200°C/400°F/Gas Mark 6.

Divide the cookie mixture into 4 portions.

Press out one portion of cookie dough into a small round cake tin. Round foil takeaway trays can also be used to good effect. Repeat the process with the remaining cookie dough if desired, or refrigerate/freeze for future use.

Place the cookie dough into the oven and bake for 6 minutes.

Reduce the oven temperature to 180°C/350°F/Gas Mark 4 and continue to bake for a further 6–8 minutes or until the dough is golden on the top and just cooked through inside.

Remove the warm cookie dough from the oven and allow to cool for 3–4 minutes before serving with vanilla ice cream.

DEEP FRIED MARS BAR

(CHIP SHOP STYLE)

Serves 1

Some may say that this dish could only have been invented in Scotland! Surprisingly light and delicious, it's a dessert that has to be tried at least once!

120 g/4 oz plain flour
60 g/2 oz cornflour
Small pinch of bicarbonate of soda
Around 200 ml/7 fl oz beer
Oil for deep frying
1 Mars bar, chilled

In a large bowl, combine the plain flour, cornflour and bicarbonate of soda. Mix well.

Slowly add the beer, whisking thoroughly until the batter becomes smooth. All of the beer may not be needed. The consistency should resemble single cream.

Heat the oil for deep-frying over a medium heat. Keep the Mars bar chilled in the fridge until ready for use.

Unwrap the Mars bar and rinse it under cold water. Dip the Mars bar into the batter until completely coated, then place carefully into the hot oil.

Deep-fry the Mars bar for 1–2 minutes or until golden on all sides. Remove from the pan and drain off any excess oil.

Place the Mars bar on a plate and slice into two pieces. The batter should be light and crisp and the Mars bar just slightly melted on the inside. Serve on its own or with ice-cream.

11

INGREDIENTS

While many excellent products are widely available in most supermarkets (and are often used by takeaway and fast-food restaurants), there are a few which are worth the effort to make from scratch. They will save you money and also offer a far superior flavour.

Fast-food restaurants go to great lengths to ensure that orders can be fulfilled quickly. To achieve this, many ingredients are pre-cooked or prepared in advance, allowing the chef to quickly create dishes full of flavour. While this is often impractical for the home cook (for example when only a small amount of a particular ingredient is desired), there are other cases where it's very much worth the time and effort of advance preparation. Where a restaurant may prepare ingredients for use that evening, we can instead store ingredients, such as garlic and ginger paste, in the freezer, so that future meals can be prepared quickly and easily.

Another reward for preparing ingredients in advance is that many dishes benefit greatly from the process. Like any good stew or casserole, a curry often tastes even better the next day. Restaurant dishes achieve this as a pleasant side effect of taking the time to pre-cook meats such as chicken and lamb tikka before reheating them to order in the final dish.

Preparing ingredients and dishes in advance makes life easier at home just as it does in the restaurant. With the groundwork done, your final dishes will often require little last-minute attention, allowing more time to relax with your guests before serving your food.

PANKO BREADCRUMBS

Makes enough breadcrumbs for around 4 chicken katsu curries

An excellent use for leftover bread and will keep well in a sealed container for several weeks. Collect and store leftover bread slices in the freezer until needed, then turn into panko breadcrumbs for a great money saver and, even more importantly, a perfect coating for any crispy chicken or fish dish.

8 slices of white bread

Preheat the oven to its lowest available setting. Arrange the bread slices on two large baking trays. Bake for around 1 hour, turning the bread slices occasionally. Ensure that the bread dries out but does not begin to brown. Remove the dried bread slices from the oven and remove the crusts. Allow the bread to cool completely. Cut each slice into 4 pieces and add to a blender. Blend for 20–30 seconds or until the bread has been turned into coarse crumbs. Store the panko breadcrumbs in a sealed container and use for any crispy chicken dish or as required in the recipes.

RESTAURANT SPICE MIX
(INDIAN RESTAURANT STYLE)

Makes enough spice mix for up to 50 curries

This creates a mix similar to that used in almost every curry dish in many Indian restaurants. It will keep well in a sealed container for 3–6 months.

8 tablespoons mild Madras curry powder
8 tablespoons paprika
8 tablespoons cumin powder
8 tablespoons coriander powder
12 tablespoons turmeric powder
4 tablespoons garam masala

In a large bowl or container, add the mild Madras curry powder, paprika, cumin powder, coriander powder, turmeric powder and garam masala. Mix thoroughly and store in a sealed container. Use as required in Indian restaurant dishes.

GARLIC AND GINGER PASTE

Makes enough paste for up to 20 curries

Using your own garlic and ginger paste in curry dishes offers a far superior flavour to shop bought varieties. It's worth the effort to make and store this paste for future use, ensuring that your hands don't have to smell of garlic every time a curry is desired!

5 garlic bulbs
1 thumb-sized piece of ginger
50 ml/2 fl oz vegetable oil
¼ teaspoon turmeric powder
Pinch of salt

Separate the garlic cloves from each bulb. Peel the garlic cloves and ginger and place in a blender with the vegetable oil. Blend well until smooth.

Heat a frying pan over a low heat. Add the garlic and ginger mixture and stir well.

Add the turmeric and salt and mix well once again. Stir-fry the paste on a low heat for around 2 minutes, or until the mixture softens and a gorgeous garlic and ginger aroma fills the room.

Remove the pan from the heat and set aside. Once the mixture is completely cool, store it in the fridge in a sealed container. Add a little extra vegetable oil if necessary to help keep the paste fresh.

The garlic and ginger paste will keep well in the fridge for several weeks or can be frozen for future use.

SWEET CHILLI SAUCE

(CHINESE TAKEAWAY STYLE)

Makes around 200 ml/7 fl oz sauce

Sweet and spicy, this can be used in various Chinese dishes, or as a dip.

2 tablespoons dry sherry
2 tablespoons fish sauce
50 ml/2 fl oz water
100 ml/4 fl oz rice wine vinegar
150 g/5 oz white sugar
2–4 teaspoons chilli flakes
1 tablespoon cornflour
2 tablespoons water

In a small pot, combine the sherry, fish sauce, water, rice wine vinegar, sugar and chilli flakes. Bring to the boil, reduce the heat to medium-low and simmer for 8–10 minutes or until the sauce is reduced. Mix the cornflour with 2 tablespoons of water and mix thoroughly. Add to the sauce and mix thoroughly again. Allow to simmer for a further 2–3 minutes or until it thickens. Serve immediately as a dip with spring rolls (page 130) or curry puffs (page 134). It will keep well in the fridge for up to 1 month.

SALT AND PEPPER SEASONING

(CHINESE TAKEAWAY STYLE)

Makes 1 small tub of salt and pepper seasoning, enough for around
4–6 portions of salt and pepper chilli chicken

1 tablespoon salt
1½ teaspoons ground Szechuan pepper
¾ teaspoon black pepper
Pinch of white pepper
¼ teaspoon Chinese 5-spice
Pinch of chilli powder

In a small bowl, add the salt, Szechuan pepper, black pepper, white pepper, Chinese 5-spice and chilli powder. Mix thoroughly. The prepared salt and pepper mixture will keep well for up to 1 month and can be used to season pork ribs, chips and chicken.

PICKLED CHILLI PEPPERS

Makes enough peppers to fill 1 x 200 ml/7 fl oz jar

These pickled chilli peppers are a great money saver and make a delicious topping to salads or kebabs.

75 g/2½ oz green and red finger chilli peppers
120 ml/4 fl oz white wine vinegar
1 garlic clove
½ bay leaf
Small pinch dried rosemary
1 teaspoon caster sugar

Cut the stems from the chilli peppers at the tip, leaving the chilli peppers sealed and unopened.

Place the chilli peppers in a small pot. Add the white wine vinegar, garlic, bay leaf, dried rosemary and caster sugar.

Stir the mixture once, bring to the boil and simmer for around 8 minutes.

Pour the pickled chilli peppers into a sterilised jam jar. Pour the remaining vinegar over the chilli peppers and add more (up to 75 ml/2½ fl oz) as needed to completely cover the chillies.

Set aside to cool completely before placing a tight fitting lid on top. Store for between 2 weeks to 1 month before use.

CHINESE STOCK

(CHINESE TAKEAWAY STYLE)

Makes around 2 litres / 3.5 pints

This simple stock can be used to extend stir-fry sauces and adds a deliciously deep background flavour to any dish.

3–4 chicken thighs (bone in)
3–4 pork spare ribs
½ small onion
2 spring onions
1 clove garlic, crushed
1 thumb sized piece of ginger, sliced
1 teaspoon soy sauce (recommended brand: Kikkoman)
2.5 litres/4½ pints water
2 tablespoons dry sherry

In a large stock pot, add the chicken thighs, pork spare ribs, onion, spring onions, garlic, ginger, soy sauce and water.

Bring the pan to boiling point over a high heat. Use a spoon to remove any foam that gathers in the middle of the pan.

Reduce the heat to low and simmer for 2–3 hours. Remove the chicken and pork pieces and strain the stock through a sieve.

Add the 2 tablespoons of dry sherry and return the pan to the heat. Simmer on low for a further 5 minutes. Set aside to cool completely and store in the fridge for up to 2 days. The stock may also be frozen in ice-cube trays and defrosted as needed in Chinese recipe dishes.

CAJUN SPICE MIX

(MEXICAN STYLE)

Makes 1 small tub, enough for around 20 Tex-Mex burgers

This mixture is so easy to prepare and far less expensive than shop bought varieties. Use for Tex-Mex burgers (page 17) or simply to coat chicken, pork or fish.

1½ teaspoons salt
½ teaspoon black pepper
1 teaspoon dried oregano
¼ teaspoon dried thyme
1 teaspoon paprika
1 teaspoon cayenne pepper
¼ teaspoon garlic powder
¼ teaspoon onion granules
¼ teaspoon cumin powder
Pinch of sugar

In a large bowl, combine the salt, black pepper, dried oregano, dried thyme, paprika, cayenne pepper, garlic powder, onion granules, cumin powder and sugar.

Mix thoroughly and store in a sealed container.

PRECOOKED CURRY CHICKEN BREAST

(INDIAN RESTAURANT STYLE)

Makes enough precooked curry chicken for 6–8 curries

Almost every Indian takeaway restaurant precooks their chicken breast, creating succulent bite sized pieces ready for use in any curry. The cooked chicken will freeze well for up to 3 months and has the added advantage of ensuring that you can create your curry dishes without the need to handle raw meat every time.

**6–8 large skinless, boneless chicken breast fillets (around
   113 g/4 oz weight per breast)**
¾ teaspoon salt
1 tablespoon lemon juice/lemon dressing
1 tablespoon tomato purée
1 tablespoon garlic and ginger paste (page 182)
½ teaspoon turmeric
¼ teaspoon chilli powder
1 tablespoon vegetable oil

Trim any excess fat from the chicken meat and cut each breast into 4–5 pieces. Add the salt and lemon juice/lemon dressing and mix well by hand. Set aside for 5 minutes.

Add the tomato purée, garlic and ginger paste, turmeric and chilli powder. Mix well again by hand and set aside for 5 minutes.

Add the vegetable oil and mix thoroughly a final time. Cover the meat and marinade for at least 4 hours, or overnight if possible.

Preheat the oven to 150°C/300°F/Gas Mark 2.

Arrange the chicken pieces on a large baking tray. Bake for around 22–24 minutes or until the chicken is tender and just cooked through.

Remove the chicken from the oven and set aside to cool. The cooked chicken pieces can be stored in the fridge for 2 days, or frozen for up to 3 months. If frozen, defrost thoroughly before use.

FOOLPROOF PRECOOKED RICE

(INDIAN RESTAURANT STYLE)

*Makes 1 portion of precooked rice (recipe may be increased provided
that ratios are kept accurate: 1 part rice / 2 parts water)*

This method of preparing rice guarantees perfect results every time. The
end result is dry, fluffy rice, perfect to serve straight away or cooled for
use in fried rice dishes.

**100 g/3½ oz good quality basmati rice per portion (uncooked
weight)**
200 ml/7 fl oz water per portion

Place the basmati rice in a large bowl and cover with plenty of cold
water. Set aside for 10 minutes.

Drain the rice and cover again with plenty of fresh, cold water. Set aside
for 20 minutes.

Drain the rice a final time and rinse through a sieve for 30 seconds,
ensuring the water runs clear.

Place the rice in a pot and add 200 ml/7 fl oz water per 100 g/3½ oz
of rice. Place the pan onto a high heat and quickly bring to the boil. Do
not stir the rice.

When the water reaches boiling point, place a tight fitting lid on the pot,
reduce the heat to the lowest available setting and simmer for 14
minutes.

Switch off the heat. Leave the pot of rice untouched for a further 10–15
minutes.

Remove the lid from the pan and use a fork to fluff up the rice. Serve
immediately or pour onto a large plate and cool as quickly as possible,
ideally within 15 minutes. A damp towel or dishcloth can be placed
underneath the plate in order to assist quick cooling.

When the rice has cooled, cover the plate with cling film and place in
the fridge for at least 4 hours, or overnight for use the next day in fried
rice dishes.

INDEX